LEVERAGE
STRENGTHENING
NEIGHBORHOODS
THROUGH DESIGN

Edited by Beth Miller and Todd Woodward

Community Design Collaborative, Philadelphia

First Edition

Copyright 2011 © The Community Design Collaborative

First published in the United States of America by
The Community Design Collaborative, Publishers
www.cdesignc.org

Editorial and project management:
Alison Rooney Communications, LLC

Design: Smyrski Creative (www.smyrskicreative.com)

Photography: Brawer & Hauptman: 111, 112
bwa architecture + planning: 5, 55, 64, 65, 73
bwa architecture + planning/Don Pearse Photographers:
70, 73
Mark Garvin: 3, 5, 17, 18, 60, 93, 101
Carryn M. Golden: 39, 69, 98
Habitat for Humanity Philadelphia: 76
Raymond W. Holman, Jr. Photography: 10, 61, 82, inside front
    and back cover
Interface Studio Architects LLC: 66, 69
Kelly/Maiello, Inc. Archtitects & Planners © Halkin
Photography LLC: 42
Peter J. Kubilis: cover, 58, 74, 75
Lager Raabe Skafte Landscape Architects, Inc.: 38, 40
Wynne Levy: 10, 15, 32, 35, 44, 49, 87, 94, 106, 109
Haley Loram: 71
Sam Oberter: 68
Spiral Q Puppet Theater: 103
Studio Agoos Lovera and Matt Wargo: 78, 79
Andrew Toy: 5, 21, 30, 35
Pablo Virgo: 104

ISBN 13: 978-0-615-52450-4

Printed and Bound in Canada by the Prolific Group

The body text is set in Whitney. The 360° sections are
set in Adobe Caslon Pro. The text is printed on two different
papers. All pages except for the 360° sections are printed on
80lb Rolland Enviro 100 Satin. The 360° sections are printed
on 80lb Starbrite Gloss. The cover is printed on 12 point
Carolina C1S with a matte film lamination.

Available through D.A.P./Distributed Art Publishers
155 Sixth Avenue, 2nd Floor, New York, N.Y. 10013
Tel: 212.627.1999 Fax: 212.627.9484

ROOF TOP SPACE
STARGAZING
CAMPING

BANDSHELL

CHURCH
FUTURE USE?

GRAY
WATER
COLLECTION

STAIRS

CONTROLLED
ACCESS

STRING
LIGHTS

DYNAMIC
SCULPTURE
GARDEN

INDUSTRIAL SITES: AN INTERIM USE CHARETTE

Green Team - Bird's Eye looking East

N Lee

Project number
2009-50
Date
10-30-2009
Scale:
1" = 10'

LEVERAGE STRENGTHENING NEIGHBORHOODS THROUGH DESIGN

6 Foreword: *The Origins of the Community Design Collaborative in Philadelphia*
Don Matzkin

8 Introduction: *Unapologetically Urban*
Beth Miller

11 *A 360° View of the Collaborative*
Maurice Cox and Alan Greenberger

12 A 360° View, Part I: *What the Collaborative Does Well*

16 *Building Toward the Public Interest: The National Significance of the Collaborative*
Jess Zimbabwe

45 A 360° View, Part II: *The Power of Design*

50 *When Is Collaboration Like Construction?*
Mark Alan Hughes

83 A 360° View, Part III: *Where the Collaborative Should Go from Here*

88 *At the Margins: Politics and Design Now*
Sally Harrison

116 *Design Is the Future*
Brian Phillips and Todd Woodward

120 *An Overview of the Collaborative*
Beth Miller

122 The Collaborative Community

126 Contributors

128 Acknowledgments

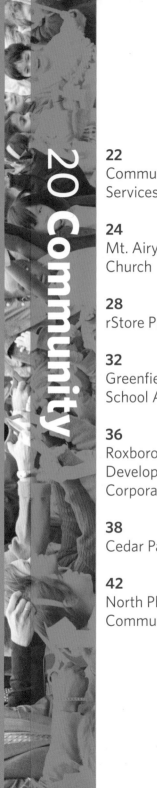

20 Community

22
Community Legal Services of Philadelphia

24
Mt. Airy Presbyterian Church

28
rStore Program

32
Greenfield Home and School Association

36
Roxborough Development Corporation

38
Cedar Park

42
North Philadelphia Community Help

54 Design

56
Oxford Street

60
The "New Angle Lounge" as "Trilogy"

62
Byron Story Foundation

66
APM at Sheridan Street

70
Mt. Tabor Cyber Village

74
Habitat for Humanity Philadelphia

78
Simons Recreation Center

92 Collaboration

94
Wynne Theater

98
Weavers Way Ogontz

102
Spiral Q Puppet Theater

106
Programs Employing People

110
Narberth Community Library

114
Allegheny West Foundaton

BY DON MATZKIN

Foreword: The Origins of the Community Design Collaborative

WE ALL KNOW HOW DIFFICULT IT IS to start anything up, much less keep it running and growing successfully for twenty years. The creation of the Collaborative was a joy from the beginning.

Inspiration was derived from the Philadelphia Architects' Workshop, an early community design workshop founded in the late 1960s by Hugh Zimmers via the Philadelphia chapter of the American Institute of Architects (AIA). In its successful early years, the Workshop was led by Hugh and longtime architectural director, the late (and much beloved) Gray Smith, an activist to the end. The mission of the Workshop was very much what we later adopted for the Collaborative: planning and design support for community groups and other nonprofit, community-based organizations in support of their efforts to bootstrap their neighborhoods.

Need was demonstrated by the Regional/Urban Design Action Team (R/UDAT) Philadelphia, a planning and design charrette sponsored by AIA National on the cusp of the 1990s that focused on rejuvenating the commercial district surrounding Amtrak's then-dilapidated North Philadelphia Station, thereby bringing widespread, much-needed attention to conditions in North Central Philly—and, by extension, many other neighborhoods of the city.

Vehicle was provided by the Young Architects Forum Philadelphia (YAF), another project of the AIA, designed to attract younger practitioners and interns to the fold, including those who had become disenchanted with what they saw as an indifference to the deteriorated physical and social conditions in our great urban centers. YAF became a vehicle for these folks to become engaged in their communities and, as a result of that engagement, to strengthen both the communities and the AIA. What better locus for the generation of an operation such as the Collaborative?

Fuel was provided by the latent energy within YAF, as well as the pent-up desire within all the design professions to **do something**.

In the Beginning

First, we invited participation from anyone who wanted in: anyone feeling they had something to contribute or just wanted to be intoxicated by the ferment. They were architects, planners, landscape architects, interior designers, graphic artists, and activists—AIA and anti-AIA. There was no set structure or established leadership. If you were there, you were an essential participant in the process and part of the leadership. Decision making followed the Quaker way of consensus.

Second, we let it take its own sweet time, meeting regularly—weekly, for a while—over the better part of two years. The first project engagement, a master plan for the expansion of a church in Southwest Philly, was conducted in the summer of 1990 by Robin Kohles, Alice Dommert, and myself. It expired, stillborn, as a result of the overreaching of a newly hired pastor, in a failed attempt to simultaneously establish and expand his turf. It taught us a valuable lesson in establishing project selection criteria.

Third, we resisted as long as possible—perhaps longer than necessary—the impulse to establish a formal structure, reveling in the creative high of anarchy in action. Leadership emerged and structure evolved organically, and the right person for a particular task never failed to step up at just the right time.

Fourth, we solicited, and received, the support of AIA Philly in the form of workspace and a modest start-up stipend. But not until we smoothed over a couple rough spots: the chapter needed to be assured that there would be no liability consequences accruing to it, and, because the YAF was an AIA project, the chapter sought control of the Collaborative. Obviously, both issues were resolved satisfactorily, with the Collaborative acquiring its own corporate status and 501(c)(3) tax designation.

Since the Beginning

The experience of the Collaborative's gestation and the aura that enveloped it at the time have carried it forward, and they are reflected today in how it performs its services, relates to clients, conducts business, governs its operation, and envisions its future. Having been only peripherally involved with the organization after its birth, it strikes me now that the Collaborative has made the most of the sense of service, interactivity, and collegiality that surrounded its founding. The special initiatives mounted by the Collaborative, for example, have been spawned by and derive their power from the neighborhood service projects that are the mainstay of the Collaborative's mission. And the relevance and authenticity of these initiatives are reinforced through the direct participation of the Collaborative's client groups.

It will only get better.

BY BETH MILLER

Introduction:
Unapologetically Urban

ONE THING WE KNOW AT THE COLLABORATIVE is that community development can be a long and tedious process. Since our founding in 1991 by a group of dedicated and self-described "anarchist architects," our portfolio has grown to include more than five hundred community-initiated projects. Of those, perhaps maybe fifty—about ten percent—have been built. Of those, most have taken five to ten years to realize.

Our services are deliberately narrow. We provide only the first ten percent of design services—an initial step that connects community groups with design professionals. We encourage groups receiving service grants to share their vision with a local task force. We also require volunteer teams to test their design interventions through peer-to-peer project reviews at mid- and final points in their conceptual design.

There is nothing more gratifying than walking by a former vacant site that has been transformed for a productive new use—such as affordable housing for seniors or a restored park—to remind you that the tedium and perseverance necessary to make the transformation was worthwhile.

We're excited to celebrate the past two decades of the Collaborative's work with this book, which details twenty projects that represent the wide variety of clients and volunteers with whom we've had the privilege of working. This volume is one way we hope to recognize the innumerable hours these dedicated professionals have spent over these past twenty years talking, looking, questioning, and designing with us. And we're constantly reinvesting the lessons learned from one project into our best efforts for the next.

The essays included here were generously contributed by some leading thinkers (and doers) in design and the evolving role of architecture today. In addition, we have interspersed excerpts from a wide-ranging conversation with Maurice Cox and Alan Greenberger, who were kind enough to share their perceptions of the Collaborative and the role of community design in our cities. We hope these excerpts inspire even more dialogues among our readers.

As Philadelphia Mayor Michael Nutter has said, design is not a luxury. Good urban design, architecture, and planning are critical to creating thriving, sustainable neighborhoods. Design can promote healthy communities by delivering built-in features that attend to specific communal needs. Public safety, commodity access, and neighborhood identity are a few of the many factors that quality design can influence significantly. Design works to reknit and revitalize urban neighborhoods.

Cities with good bones and infrastructure are the ultimate canvas for sustainable initiatives. Over the past sixty years, public policy has tended to direct investment outside urban centers. After six decades of shrinking, Philadelphia's population decline has stabilized and we're beginning to grow again. The city is taking advantage of this momentum by investing in zoning reform and in Philadelphia 2035—the first comprehensive plan in a generation.

Design is not the only factor at play in our neighborhoods, but it is a critical tool for evaluating ways to turn obstacles into assets. Even more importantly, community design—integrating planning and design services with community development—further engages residents, businesses, government representatives, and nonprofits as advocates for quality places to work, play, learn, worship, and thrive. We're proud to continue our work toward this end, and feel fortunate to have had the opportunity over the past two decades in the life of this city—and this country—to do our part.

Beth Miler (top left) is Executive Director of the Community Design Collaborative.

Alan Greenberger (bottom left) is Deputy Mayor for Planning and Economic Development and Director of Commerce for the City of Philadelphia.

Todd Woodward (top right) is an architect and member of the Collaborative's Advisory Council.

Maurice Cox (bottom right) is Associate Professor at the University of Virginia's School of Architecture, the former mayor of Charlottesville, Virginia, and former Director of Design for the National Endowment for the Arts.

For detailed bios, see p. 126.

A 360° View of the Collaborative

On March 8, 2011, the Community Design Collaborative's Executive Director Beth Miller and Advisory Council member Todd Woodward sat down for a roundtable discussion with Alan Greenberger and Maurice Cox, to draw upon their local and national expertise in architecture, urban planning, and community design. The conversation focused on the Collaborative and its impact—past, present, and future—and the potential roles for similar organizations within urban environments.

Rather than presenting the ideas that emerged in the form of an essay, we offer here—in three sections, throughout the book—a series of excerpts from that conversation. The excerpts are organized by topic, which include: **What the Collaborative Does Well** (Connecting the Grassroots with the Grass Tops, Supporting Commercial Corridors, and Translating Lessons Learned); **The Power of Design** (Building Political Awareness, Tackling Problems as Designers, Approaches to Infill Housing, and Design versus Implementation); and **Where the Collaborative Should Go from Here** (The Project-Formation Business, Making Cities the Client, Seizing Philadelphia's "Planning Moment," and Institutionalizing Good Design). We hope that within these threads of conversation you will see resonances with the essays and project profiles.

A 360° View, Part I: *What the Collaborative Does Well*

Connecting the Grass Roots with the Grass Tops

*Todd Woodward: **How do you see the Collaborative increasing the role of design in the city?***

Maurice Cox: I have talked about a grass-roots, incremental approach, using Philadelphia as a laboratory to get things done and to show some capacity. **There is so much to be gained by doing hundreds of small experiments**—versus waiting for the overarching vision that takes a multi-million-dollar, community-wide initiative.

All of **these small projects build the community's confidence** that change can happen, and it can happen in a place where they can see it. I'm a big advocate for a kind of grass-roots design activism: at the end of five years, let's see what we've done. At the end of ten years, let's see all of the work.

On the other side, for the more robust and visionary large-scale transformations, that comes as a result of a lot of collaboration on the part of a community. So every time [community members] get together to talk about intervention on a block, they're building their ability to talk about larger, more challenging undertakings. For that, inevitably, politicians need community support, in order to have the political will to implement stuff that will be transformative and is going to ruffle a lot of people's feathers.

All of these smaller things that happen at the neighborhood level that support excellence in the built environment and quality of life, build a capacity for our political leaders to make the big steps, whether it's reanimating a waterfront, creating a mega park system or re-greening the city: things that take a real vision. That capacity has to be built, and the community has to be in the habit of having that conversation. It has to be a conversation.

I'm a big believer in putting things out in the community that force people to step up and engage. Even if it doesn't get implemented, the act of having discussed this stuff publicly is so vital to building up their capacity to accept the change.

A key role that a design center plays is to keep that conversation going, to keep issues that are challenging for communities in their face, and keep them at the table, and at the same time implementing these small changes that they see around them every day, or every month. That's how you create a vibrant, community-wide discussion.

Beth Miller: It's like a series of steady drips, and then someone who can help connect all of that. We talk about joining the grass roots and the grass tops.

Supporting Commercial Corridors

*Todd: **How can our support for local businesses impact entire neighborhoods?***

Alan Greenberger: In Philadelphia, there are dozens of neighborhood commercial corridors; some have a regional flavor, and they vary in quality. But they all grew to a size that was consistent with the higher population base fifty years ago, and as the population has decreased in many of them, the demand for the commercial activity over, say, five blocks now could be compressed into three. This is something the Collaborative could help with: [one of the City's] important initiatives, to help communities understand the value of and work toward 100 percent occupancy in those three blocks, and how this is better than 60 percent occupancy over five blocks.

Maurice: There is an enormous opportunity to reinforce local retail and to create more proximity and synergy around locally supported businesses, and support centers for entrepreneurship, as opposed to an urban Target model. So many cities look for big bang, as opposed to the fine-grained, one-off, quirky neighborhood character that comes from getting people involved in local businesses.

A lot of neighborhood centers and commercial corridors have been strung out, are too long, and generally are not a good walk, because of the high vacancy. So what are other adaptive uses for those storefronts that would lead to a local vibrant area? **It hinges on the locally owned, grass-roots creation of a neighborhood and neighborhood character.** But it's challenging to find localities that embrace things that are locally driven and small-focused [with] local entrepreneurship, if that is our economic development strategy.

Alan: The nature of those local businesses and the health of those local corridors are a source of great pride for people, even if their shopping patterns might take them to three different ones…. Even in healthy neighborhoods, Americans don't shop the way we used to for food or medicine. People have choices; even low-income residents have cars, and will use them to go to where they want to shop….

The source of pride of communities is attached to what does survive: restaurants, cultural facilities, at least in [my neighborhood of] Mt. Airy. Others we've thought of as problematic to the core but in fact can be used to support [the neighborhood]. For example, a community acupuncture practice in Mt. Airy has put together street-worthy presence. He's a

careful shopkeeper who takes care of his property and is concerned about the well-being of the pizza guy next door. Management of these corridors and thinking about retail strategies are different from how we used to think about them; there are new players who are (and are not) now in the mix. Not every corridor is going to have a supermarket.

Beth: But every corridor might have an architect—a small firm.

Alan: Certainly they would have professional services such as accountants, lawyers—things that traditionally turned up on the second floor might end up on the first floor, in the right mix. Along with street-oriented businesses: the restaurant, the pizza shop, the liquor store. There is a lot of attention that needs to be paid to that sort of thing, because when you get it right—even though people are shopping all over—they are great community builders, and they make people feel like the community has something going for it.

At the residential level, [it has a huge impact] if you get half the people on the block to tend to a tree, put out a flower box, put a flag up. On a random block of [North Philadelphia on] 8th Street between Dauphin and Susquehanna, someone has organized [the residents]. They took vacant lots and cleaned them up, and now use the street for block parties. On a Sunday, everyone is out cleaning their white stoops, and everyone has flags hanging over the door. It looks great. And you think, "This block is totally under control, and it didn't have anything to do with government." The next block—which has no such organization—looks dramatically different, even though it has the same infrastructure.

Beth: **Those small-scale interventions are critical for organizing and preparing the community** for future implementations.

Translating Lessons Learned

Todd: *We're curious about how the model of what the Collaborative has done in Philadelphia might apply to other cities and areas. What are your thoughts about how what we do here is applicable (or not)?*

Maurice: **There are very few places in any community—of a variety of sizes—where community, development, and city interests can meet and have honest and frank discussions** about the potential of projects. By the time you get into the city process, you're well into the regulatory process. Very often some vision is already set in stone.

Centers like the Collaborative offer a place where the public can deliberate the values they may have, [which helps] developers begin to understand what a particular community stands for. My experience is that city planning departments generally don't have a lot of time for reflective planning, because they're charged with managing the regulatory process, which is about getting projects implemented. So community design centers are a place where they can reflect, long before responding to a development parcel.

We don't have enough such places in communities, and yet they should be hand in hand with city planning departments. My experience has been that, where you have a robust design community, in terms of professionals as well as advocates, you have a high level of design excellence.

Alan Greenberger: As I've crossed over from teaching in architecture to teaching in planning, I [find I] love the latter, because students come to planning with a background and expertise in multiple disciplines. They intuitively know how to work together to solve a problem. At Penn when we put together teams to look after a project, we want an economics person, a transportation person, a community development person, a real estate person— all from different worlds. The results have been fabulous. Where they tend to be weak is, actually, in design.

Maurice: I share your sense that **to solve problems [and] build the natural environment, you need a cross section of disciplines.** When I managed the Mayors' Institute on City Design, the teams we brought in to advise mayors represented at least six different disciplines, that went from urban design, urban planning, landscape architecture, architecture, transportation, transportation engineering, real estate development, even downtown management know-how, because **problems are complex and multilayered**, and each discipline brings deep knowledge.

When you overlap those, you get highly sophisticated responses. It's not necessarily how we go about planning our cities—much to our detriment. But that's another advantage of having a design collaborative: you're able to bring different disciplines to the table.

Alan: This may be a place where the Collaborative could extend this idea beyond design

to other disciplines that are interested in development: reaching out to the real estate community, the legal community, and certainly the planning community.

Beth: That model of interdisciplinary teams is something we do with all of our service grants: landscape architect, engineer, planner, architect, preservationists. Taking that one step further, we've been able to test [the model] with Infill Philadelphia. As a follow-up to our industrial sites, we'll do an Urban Land Institute technical assistance program to help test the financial feasibility of the proposal.

Alan: It would be interesting to compress and integrate that into a single team; design in context of implementation.

Beth: **Everyone has a common goal to improve the city**; it's just how to get these different audiences to communicate around what it is and could be; what's possible, what's pragmatic. Our design teams learn as much from clients as clients learn from them. There remains this perception of the developers as the bad guys, so we work with the nonprofit developers first, and next we will reach out to private-sector developers.

Maurice: You can't do this kind of transformative work without the development community at the table. I don't see them as an entity that has to come at some subsequent stage; they are critical to being able to talk about the economic viability of even some of the more visionary ideas that might be proposed in their absence.

Beth: That's the next frontier.

Maurice: **I've come to value the bottom line**

know-how about an idea. I like the notion of having various disciplines—especially those who can talk about the history of a place, because so many of the places we're talking about have been changed and transformed over time. If you have history, you gain an authority, but also a way to talk to a broad cross section of stakeholders who have seen changes in the built environment over time, whether it's preservation or interpretation of the place, because no urban site is without a lengthy history.

Alan: You might go into a block where the problem isn't solely a vision for the block; it's also that it's not managed well, or people haven't organized themselves to take certain initiatives that are fairly doable: to plant trees, clean up vacant lots. This is a time where, through heightened sensitivity of the design community, or integration of people from somewhat different perspectives, [the Collaborative] can provide a team that says: here are the essential things we need to do to get to this vision—raise money, build capacity, clean up the block, and so on. And there are techniques and linkages to operations that know how to do that and can help you with it.

Beth: We've found that, by providing service grants to nonprofits and responding to their requests, we get automatic buy-in. Sometimes they're not quite ready for that level of engagement, but the process is a form of community organizing that gets people rallied around a cause together, and the stakeholder and the task forces that are a part of our process help reinforce that. Sometimes the design professional is the external party that everybody throws the darts at; strange bedfellows can come together on that. I see that as valuable community development.

BY JESS ZIMBABWE

Building Toward the Public Interest: The National Significance of the Collaborative

The people I love the best
jump into work head first
without dallying in the shallows
and swim off with sure strokes almost out of sight.

...

I love people who harness themselves, an ox to a heavy cart,
who pull like water buffalo, with massive patience,
who strain in the mud and the muck to move things forward,
who do what has to be done, again and again.

...

who are not parlor generals and field deserters
but move in a common rhythm
when the food must come in or the fire be put out.

—*Marge Piercy, from* To Be of Use[1]

THE WORK OF CITIZEN PARTICIPATION IN DESIGN AND PLANNING decisions takes place in crowded gymnasiums, cafeterias, coffee shops, and commission hearing rooms throughout the country. With few exceptions, all parties enter the process—design professionals, officials of the sponsoring or responsible public agency, neighbors, developers, and community activists—with an intention to build the best project possible. But as anyone who has ever attended a community meeting can tell you, the resulting process can be far from civil. I have heard epithets yelled, seen fists drawn, and witnessed professional actors exposed for accepting pay to play the role of neighborhood residents. It is fair to say that the real challenge of our era of diminished civic trust is to shift the paradigm of the system from the "expert/professional" model to one that actually—and adeptly—seeks and incorporates community input into decisions.

As President of the Association for Community Design, I studied models of community design centers across the country and even internationally, and in my current position at the Urban Land Institute's Daniel Rose Center for Public Leadership in Land Use, I work with mayors, city councilmembers, planning and transportation directors, and dozens of other leaders in local government (including a team of Daniel Rose Fellows from Philadelphia that included Mayor Michael Nutter). I believe the Community Design Collaborative in Philadelphia has developed the single-best model for sustained and impactful volunteer work by design professionals on real community needs, and fully deserves the praise it has received from its peers across the country.

The Collaborative works to transcend not only the typical economic relationship of design services, but also the limitations of the roles that normally circumscribe participants. Through service grants that pair talented professionals with deserving community-based nonprofits, the Collaborative helps all participants to examine how to break out of the typical roles of activist, politician, community member, and designer.

Jumping in Head First: Identifying and Then Solving Problems

"Dreams can become reality, and we are so appreciative of [the Collaborative] supplying us with a first step on our quest to have

Perhaps the clearest example of the Collaborative's work in this realm of effectively engaging citizens in broader policy debates is the Infill Philadelphia initiative. By creating speculative designs for real sites, the Collaborative engaged stakeholders in policy issues that would otherwise have remained inaccessible to them. The conceptual designs developed for Infill Philadelphia were created through a "design challenge," an intensive, interactive design process in which volunteer design firms worked simultaneously to develop conceptual ideas for three real-life sites selected by community-based organizations. The first phase of the initiative focused on affordable housing, and the resulting volunteer-driven, speculative designs during that phase gained the attention of the Pennsylvania Housing Finance Agency. After experiencing the powerful design work of the Collaborative's volunteers, the agency included design quality as a criteria in the Excellence in Design Initiative, a special round of funding for projects applying for housing tax credits.

the quality of our physical space match the quality of the educational program we have been providing over the last 43 years."

> —Sarah A. Dorbian, Director, Overbrook Preschool and Kindergarten, March 16, 2010

Most patently, the Collaborative provides direct and useful service to deeply worthy community-based nonprofits that benefit from the improved facilities made possible in part by the Collaborative's services. Mission-driven nonprofits are not experts in facility development. Most organizations of the type that the Collaborative serves will only undertake a single facility development or redevelopment project, if they do so at all. Often, the dedicated staff of these organizations are so focused on the urgent tasks at hand—finding shelter for the homeless, protecting victims of domestic violence, providing literacy skills—that they seldom stop even to consider their facility needs. When the staff do consider these needs, they usually acknowledge a gross inadequacy in their existing facility but see any funds spent on expanding or improving their space as a zero-sum game, feeling instead that funds need to be dedicated directly to advancing their mission.

Gaining the expert advice of a trained design professional can

be extraordinarily valuable, then, in allowing them to remain focused on their mission. The Collaborative doesn't just partner with these clients; it educates them to see how design can *reflect* their mission—how investing in their work environment can yield dramatic increases in efficiency, employee and volunteer satisfaction, and a sense of pride and ownership for employees, volunteers, and clients served.

Swimming with Sure Strokes:
Positioning Both Client and Volunteer

When the Collaborative initiates a pairing between a designer/volunteer and a nonprofit organization, it carefully evaluates potential projects and nonprofit clients through a written application, a site visit, a client interview, and review by a selection committee (which includes architects, landscape architects, construction managers, economic development experts, real estate developers, an attorney, and representatives of the public sector). This ensures that the projects to which the Collaborative asks its volunteers to donate their services are credible, address pressing urban development issues, and involve work with clients and communities that are prepared to benefit from pre-design assistance.

The Collaborative's pre-screening also ensures a more

Gaining the expert advice of a trained design professional can be extraordinarily valuable ... in allowing [nonprofits] to remain focused on their mission.

meaningful experience for volunteers than do projects that individuals would be likely to find on their own. Designers who seek a worthy pro bono client often learn the hard (and time-consuming) way that many worthy nonprofit organizations are not ready to engage a designer. For all of the training, education, and experience that architects get in *solving* problems, they are not always the most adept at *identifying* problems—a skill set that traditional architectural education has under-emphasized. For some thirty worthwhile nonprofit facility projects each year, the Collaborative helps fill this gap with pre-development services.

Moving Things Forward:
Affecting the Profession of Architecture

Forty-three years ago, when Whitney Young, Jr. spoke before the annual convention of the American Institute of Architects in Portland, he excoriated the profession for doing too little to engage with the crises that were facing American cities in 1968:

> "As a profession, you [have] not distinguished [your-self] by your social and civic contributions to the cause of civil rights, and I am sure this has not come to you as any shock. You are most distinguished by your thunderous silence and your complete irrelevance."[2]

In the years since, architects and their professional organizations have come a long way, creating dozens of community design centers that serve the needs of nonprofit organizations and underserved communities across the country. But the fact remains that within the larger profession of architecture, public interest design is still a marginalized mode of service delivery. In 1996, a seminal Carnegie Foundation report on the state of architectural education concluded that "schools of architecture could do more ... to instill in students a commitment to lives of engagement and service."[3]

Community design, with its focus on delivering a useful service, downplays the popular myth of heroic architects employing abstract design ideas in novel ways. To a public that is skeptical that architects contribute anything besides elitist abstractions, community design centers present a potent counterargument of committed architects who can listen to the community and effectively communicate—without jargon—with their clients and the public at large. The Collaborative, founded in 1991, was certainly a pioneer in this arena. By providing unique professional exposure for volunteer designers—and especially professionals early in their careers—the Collaborative normalizes pro bono design practice, making it more palatable and comprehendible to mainstream practitioners.

For emerging architects committed to public service, volunteering with the Collaborative creates opportunities to demonstrate leadership in ways that traditional architectural practice does not:

> "Volunteering energizes me and allows me to stay passionate about what I do."
> —Natalie Malawey-Eddie, AIA, RMJM

"Having the opportunity to stand on your own two feet and see a project through early on in your career is very healthy. Young designers need to have new experiences to grow, which includes opportunities to engage directly with clients, lead a project, and present your project to great design professionals."
  —*Mami Hara, Principal, Wallace, Roberts & Todd LLC*

"We are attracted by the complexity of the issues and the chance to work with diverse groups of people."
  —*Charles Loomis, AIA, and Chariss McAfee, AIA*[4]

They are forced to be more independent and entrepreneurial, learning simultaneously the professional competencies of an architectural internship as they begin to grasp the complexities of their daily lives as public service–oriented interns.

These benefits are especially important to designers who are just starting out in the field. By volunteering as a part of a Collaborative project, early career professionals gain exposure to key aspects of the preliminary phase of the design, including programming, site analysis, schematic design, code research, and material research. They also have an opportunity to take a leadership role in project management activities such as team coordination, client relations, and presentations.

Moving in a Common Rhythm: Building Knowledge for Collective Impacts
To a casual observer of the Collaborative, it is not readily apparent that their work raises awareness about the importance of design in support of bigger urban policy efforts. There are tremendous knock-on effects of a single coordinated entity like the Collaborative undertaking twenty years of projects, with the institutional memory and resources to knit them all together. At its simplest, this suggests another role for the architect besides that of a design service provider.

We tend to think of ourselves as citizens of a nation-state (because that's who issues our passports and processes our duty-free purchases), but we define most *daily* practices of citizenship—voting, public education, jury duty, paying a parking ticket—within our local community. However, our representative system of government has meant the rise of a political class of elected and appointed decision makers who are occupied full-time with the act of governing—and therefore necessarily divorced from the day-to-day operations of commerce, culture, industry, services, and urban development.

A study by the Kettering Foundation shows what we would expect: public officials *want* better relationships with citizens, but found that citizen engagement creates delays and red tape. The same study shows that citizens feel like their concerns won't be heard unless they organize into angry groups.[5] The Collaborative serves as an intermediary at exactly these two points of entry: in providing citizens (clients) with the tools/language/documentation they need to communicate with and be heard by public officials, as well as providing public officials with the context and the relationships they need to work effectively to satisfy their constituents.

Every city in the country would benefit from an organization that serves the role the Collaborative does in Philadelphia. Through its institutional strength, longevity, and capacity, the Collaborative brings what it has learned from a long list of successful (and some unsuccessful) projects to bear on neighborhood-, community- and city-wide discussions of policy and practice. Revealing how architects can effectively facilitate groups, organize communities, manage facility projects, and develop real estate, the Collaborative demonstrates a more complete skill set for the architecture profession—one that should serve as a model at the national level.

1 From *Circles on the Water* (Alfred A. Knopf, Inc. and Middlemarsh, Inc., 1982).
2 The entire 1968 Whitney Young, Jr. address to the AIA can be found at: http://isites.harvard.edu/fs/docs/icb.topic753413.files/14_Outsiders%20in%20the%20Profession/Young%201968%20AIA%20speech.pdf
3 Boyer, Ernest L. and Lee D. Mitgang, *Building Community: A New Future for Architecture Education and Practice* (Stanford, CA: Carnegie Foundation for the Advancement of Teaching, 1996), 129–42.
4 Volunteer testimonials provided by the Collaborative.
5 The Kettering Foundation, "Public Administrators and Citizens: What Should the Relationship Be?" (Dayton, OH: Author, January 2007). Retrieved 5/29/11 from http://www.kettering.org/media_room/publications/public_administrators_and_citizens

Connecting design professionals to community groups and neighborhoods that might not otherwise benefit from design services has always been a key tenet of the Collaborative. This section highlights projects that have had an explicit impact on a neighborhood, brought community groups together, or could serve as prototypes for addressing broader citywide issues.

Leverage: Strengthening Neighborhoods through Design

21

A new way in: Before (lower right), CLS worked out of two adjacent storefronts. A key goal for the new design (center) was to create a more welcoming, accessible entrance.

Letting in the Light:
Community Legal Services of Philadelphia

The Collaborative's design team helped CLS envision a new building that would better serve its low-income clients in the North Philadelphia neighborhood where the center had long been a critical resource.

Responding to Specific Needs

CLS was particularly vocal about its desire for offices with natural light, and in response the team created a U-shaped building footprint, which shaped the ultimate design of this project, which is under construction in 2011.

The staff needed meeting spaces where clients would have privacy to discuss confidential matters, which was also lacking in their current space. They also wanted meeting spaces that could serve the law center and the community. All of these features support CLS's goal of expanding its client base. The plans allowed CLS to mobilize quickly to raise funds and hire a project team.

Location
1402-12 West Erie Ave. (at Broad St.), North Philadelphia

Services completed
2009

Client
Community Legal Services of Philadelphia (CLS)

Volunteers
Jibe Design; JxN Studio, LLC; Bittenbender Construction

Hours donated (value)
375 ($30,710)

Products
Programming study, preliminary code review, conceptual design, preliminary cost estimate

Sustainable design features
Daylighting, energy-efficient heating systems (photovoltaic panels, geothermal heat pumps, radiant floor heating)

Consultant for final design
Atkin Olshin Schade Architects

Built
Construction scheduled to begin in 2011

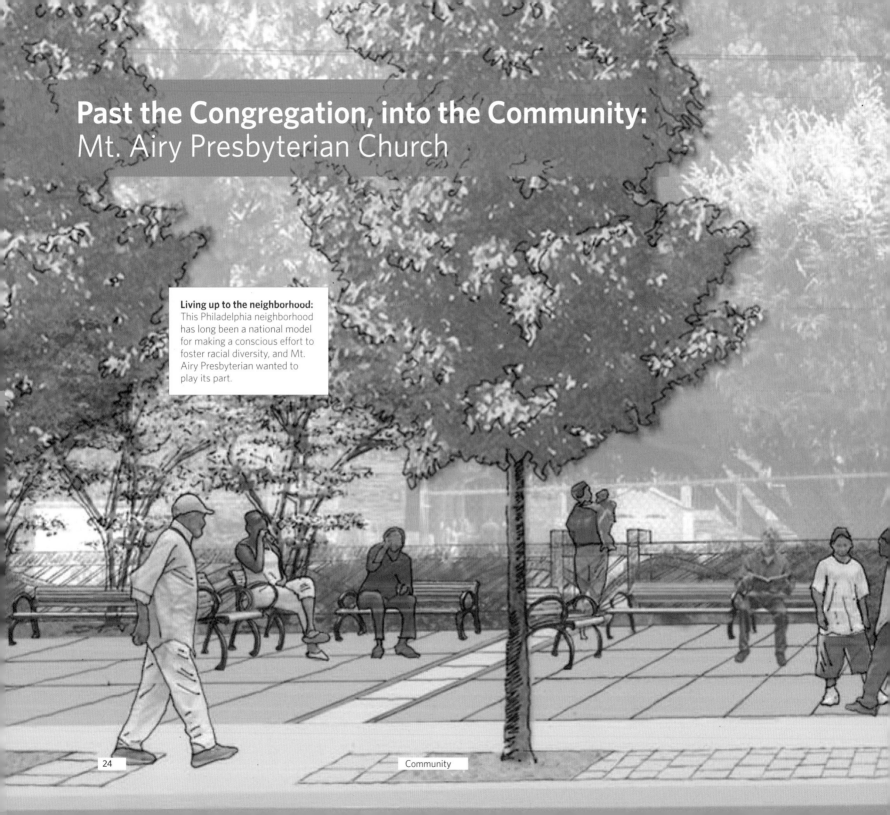

Past the Congregation, into the Community:
Mt. Airy Presbyterian Church

Living up to the neighborhood:
This Philadelphia neighborhood has long been a national model for making a conscious effort to foster racial diversity, and Mt. Airy Presbyterian wanted to play its part.

Location
13 East Mt. Pleasant Ave. (at Germantown Ave.), Mt. Airy neighborhood, Philadelphia

Services completed
2008

Client
Mt. Airy Presbyterian Church

Volunteers
Owner's Rep, Inc.; Kate Brower; Justin DiPietro, RLA; David Boelker

Hours donated (value)
169 ($16,360)

Products
Conceptual design, preliminary cost estimate, phasing plan, maintenance plan

Built
No

Over the years, several churches have approached the Collaborative about doing master plans. But Mt. Airy Presbyterian Church had a unique request. It had already brought the larger community inside the church by offering space to local organizations. Now the congregation wanted to rethink its outdoor space—a large lawn facing the commercial corridor of Germantown Avenue—to engage the community even more.

Improving on function:
Currently the church presents merely a functional front on the Germantown Avenue Commercial Corridor.

"[Since] 1997, commercial corridor activities in Mt. Airy have attracted more than $40 million in private investment, some 40 new storefront businesses, 175 new jobs, and stabilized property values .... [these] accomplishments are considered a national standard bearer for CDC-led commercial corridor revitalization."
—Mt. Airy USA website

Sharing the Front Yard

The church sought to support the ambitious and successful revitalization and community reinvestment efforts already underway for this corridor by Mt. Airy USA, a nearby community development corporation. Mt. Airy USA was seeking to develop and restore storefronts and streetscapes along Germantown Avenue to reverse the blight visited upon the area in previous decades.

The resulting plan sought to carve out a piece of the lawn, used primarily as a daycare play yard, and repurpose it for a gathering space that the entire community could use. This would create a pause along the reviving corridor.

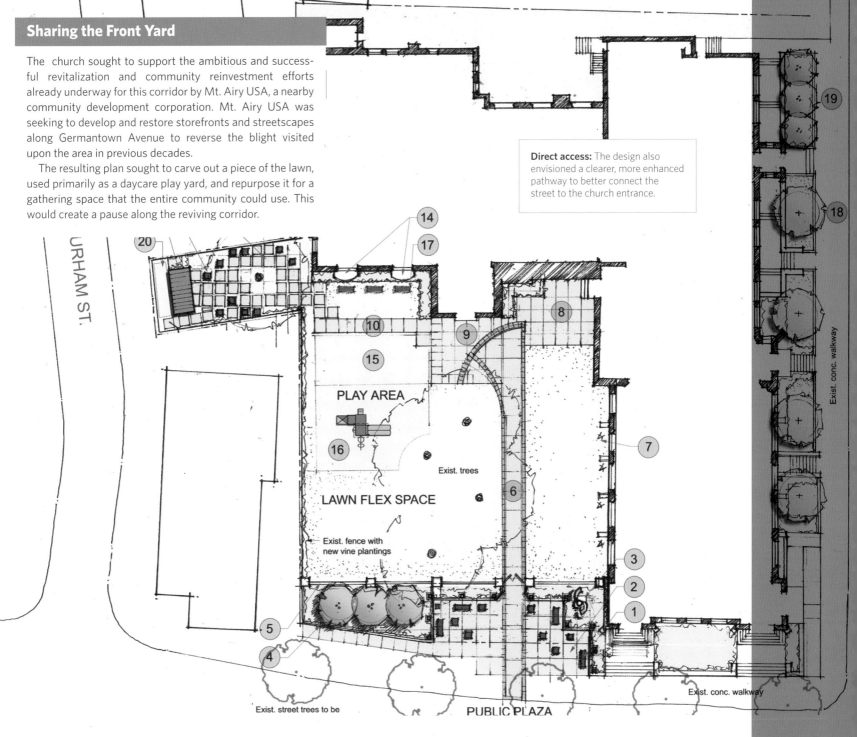

Direct access: The design also envisioned a clearer, more enhanced pathway to better connect the street to the church entrance.

URHAM ST.

PLAY AREA

LAWN FLEX SPACE

Exist. trees

Exist. fence with new vine plantings

Exist. street trees to be

PUBLIC PLAZA

Exist. conc. walkway

Exist. conc. walkway

Changing the Face of Commercial Corridors:
rStore Program

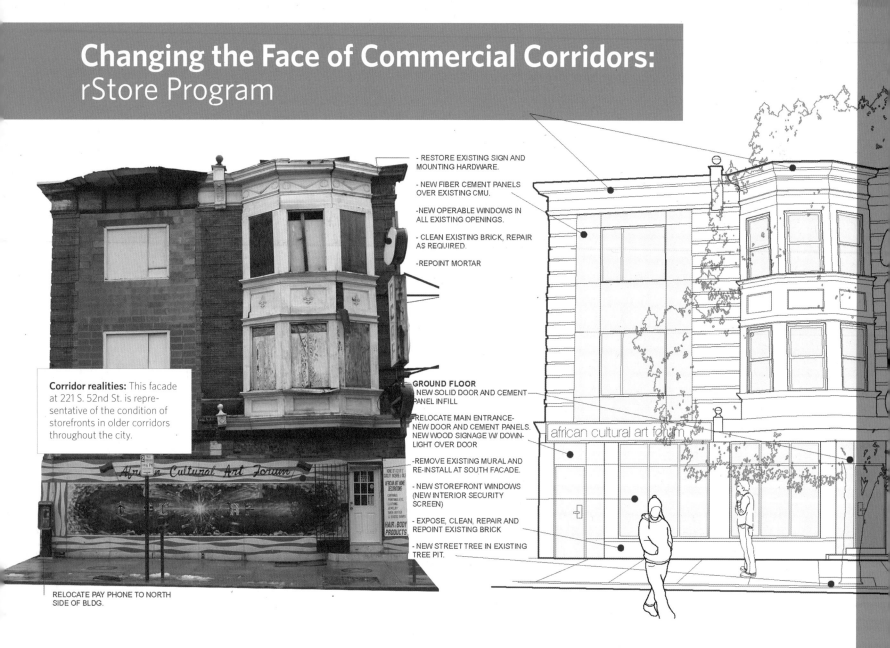

Corridor realities: This facade at 221 S. 52nd St. is representative of the condition of storefronts in older corridors throughout the city.

- RESTORE EXISTING SIGN AND MOUNTING HARDWARE.

- NEW FIBER CEMENT PANELS OVER EXISTING CMU.

- NEW OPERABLE WINDOWS IN ALL EXISTING OPENINGS.

- CLEAN EXISTING BRICK, REPAIR AS REQUIRED.

- REPOINT MORTAR

GROUND FLOOR
- NEW SOLID DOOR AND CEMENT PANEL INFILL

- RELOCATE MAIN ENTRANCE-NEW DOOR AND CEMENT PANELS. NEW WOOD SIGNAGE W/ DOWNLIGHT OVER DOOR

- REMOVE EXISTING MURAL AND RE-INSTALL AT SOUTH FACADE.

- NEW STOREFRONT WINDOWS (NEW INTERIOR SECURITY SCREEN)

- EXPOSE, CLEAN, REPAIR AND REPOINT EXISTING BRICK

- NEW STREET TREE IN EXISTING TREE PIT.

african cultural art forum

RELOCATE PAY PHONE TO NORTH SIDE OF BLDG.

These projects build on the premise that "good design is good business." What started out as an individual service grant to a community development corporation grew into a series of "design days" to help neighborhood merchants improve their storefronts. Ultimately these relationships led to the Collaborative delivering a broad base of design services through an ongoing relationship with the City's Commerce Department.

Location
Various. One example opposite: 221 South 52nd St. (at Walnut St.), West Philadelphia

Services completed
2008

Client
The Enterprise Center CDC

Volunteers
International Consultants, Inc.; Andrew Cronin; Kate Czembor, AIA; Shaun Patchel

Hours donated (value)
82 ($9,055)

Products
Three design consultations with business owners, conceptual drawings

Built
No

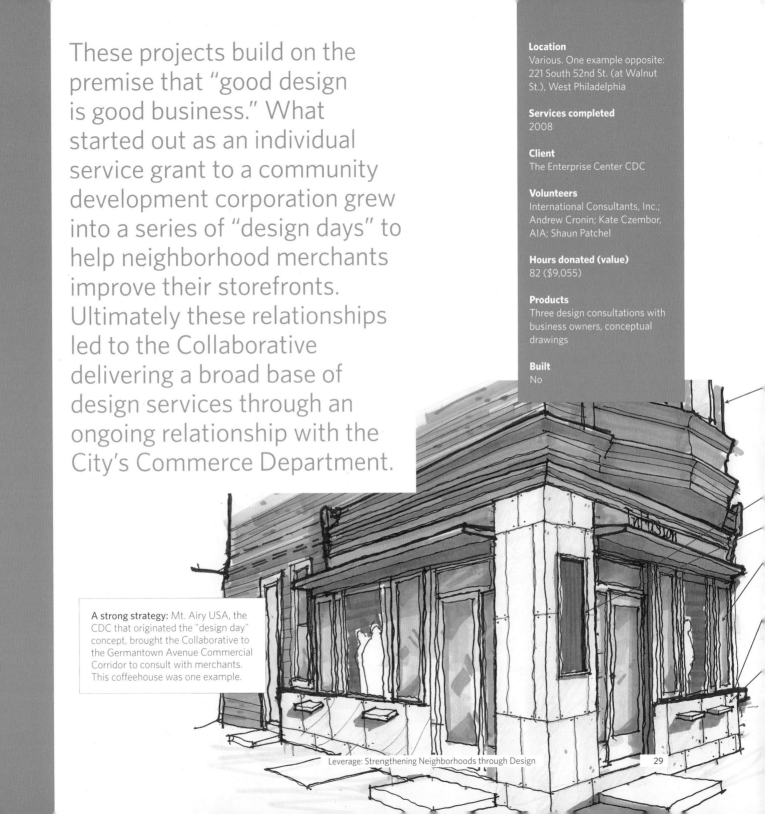

A strong strategy: Mt. Airy USA, the CDC that originated the "design day" concept, brought the Collaborative to the Germantown Avenue Commercial Corridor to consult with merchants. This coffeehouse was one example.

A New Focus on Facelifts

Over the past decade, the Commerce Department began working more strategically to target investment with its Storefront Improvement Program (SIP), which offers funding to business owners to invest in their buildings. At the same time, The Merchants Fund had reinvented itself as a source for grants to small businesses, including business owners looking for matching grants for storefront renovations.

Design Days

The collaboration had begun in 2005 with Mt. Airy USA, a Northwest Philadelphia–based community development corporation charged with improving the Germantown Avenue Commercial Corridor. The CDC recruited storeowners and paired them with architects for a one-on-one design consult. In 2006, other CDCs began referring storeowners to the Collaborative for conceptual drawings for facade improvements that addressed improvement priorities, cost, building and zoning regulations, and sidewalk appeal.

An Evolving Role

The Collaborative's contract with the City has continued to evolve. In addition to troubleshooting with SIP grant recipients during implementation, the Collaborative now sits on the City's SIP Design Review Team, along with members with retail and economic development expertise. The Collaborative helps to recognize successful store investment projects citywide, organizing Philadelphia's first Citywide Storefront Challenge and a design workshop for corridor managers.

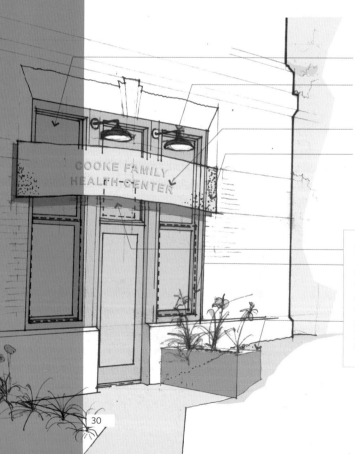

Cooke Family Health Center facelift: In 2011 Logan CDC referred this community health center to the Collaborative, which recommended a number of low-cost, high-impact changes: old signage and security grilles (right) replaced with a new projecting sign, lighting, a planter, and brighter paint (left).

Community

Talking facades: Design consultations like this one, with a Frankford Avenue Commercial Corridor merchant in 2009, support storeowners in taking the time, energy, and—sometimes—the leap of faith required to reinvest in their facades.

Unpaving a Playground:
Greenfield Home and School Association

Fun and practical: Four phases were devised to support the school association's fund-raising, each one complementing Greenfield's new environmental curriculum. Phase two involved forming mounds covered in porous rubber that absorb stormwater runoff.

Location
22nd and Chestnut Sts.,
Center City Philadelphia

Services completed
2009

Client
Greenfield Home and School
Association (HSA)

Volunteers
Kling Stubbins

Products
Existing conditions report,
conceptual design, proposed
phasing, and opinion of probable
cost

Consultant for final design
SMP Architects;
Viridian Landscape Studio;
Meliora Environmental Design,
LLC

Built
2009

"Greening Greenfield" transformed a "hot, noisy, and hard-surfaced" Center City schoolyard into a model green facility and outdoor classroom. The design represented the first instance of retrofitting an existing public school campus in Philadelphia. The outcome also planted seeds of change for parent- and teacher-led campus greening efforts at other public and charter schools.

For cars more than kids: Before, much of the playground was paved with asphalt and used as a parking lot.

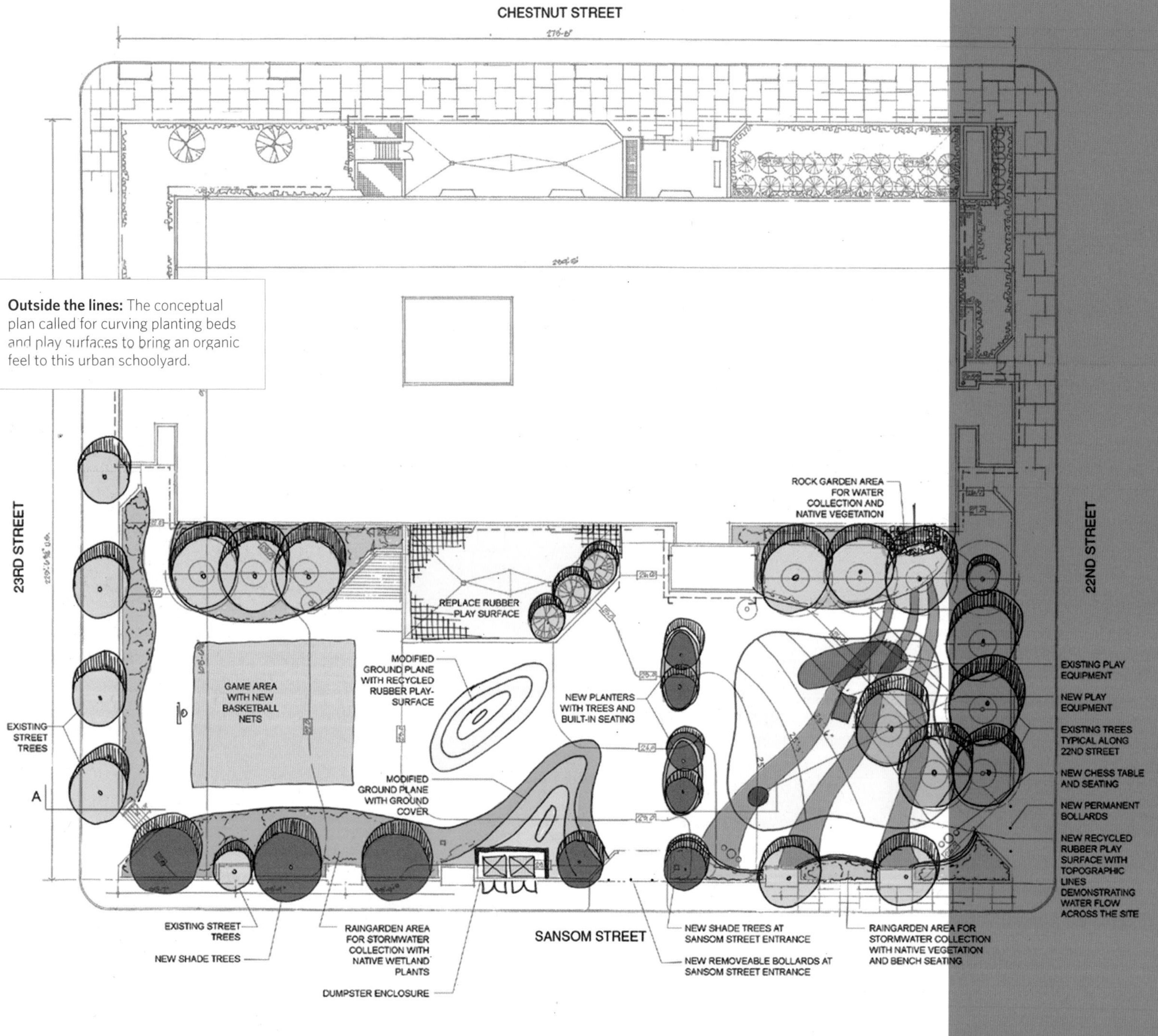

CHESTNUT STREET

Outside the lines: The conceptual plan called for curving planting beds and play surfaces to bring an organic feel to this urban schoolyard.

23RD STREET

22ND STREET

ROCK GARDEN AREA
FOR WATER
COLLECTION AND
NATIVE VEGETATION

REPLACE RUBBER
PLAY SURFACE

EXISTING
STREET
TREES

GAME AREA
WITH NEW
BASKETBALL
NETS

MODIFIED
GROUND PLANE
WITH RECYCLED
RUBBER PLAY-
SURFACE

NEW PLANTERS
WITH TREES AND
BUILT-IN SEATING

EXISTING PLAY
EQUIPMENT

NEW PLAY
EQUIPMENT

EXISTING TREES
TYPICAL ALONG
22ND STREET

NEW CHESS TABLE
AND SEATING

A

MODIFIED
GROUND PLANE
WITH GROUND
COVER

NEW PERMANENT
BOLLARDS

NEW RECYCLED
RUBBER PLAY
SURFACE WITH
TOPOGRAPHIC
LINES
DEMONSTRATING
WATER FLOW
ACROSS THE SITE

EXISTING STREET
TREES

NEW SHADE TREES

RAINGARDEN AREA
FOR STORMWATER
COLLECTION WITH
NATIVE WETLAND
PLANTS

DUMPSTER ENCLOSURE

SANSOM STREET

NEW SHADE TREES AT
SANSOM STREET ENTRANCE

NEW REMOVEABLE BOLLARDS AT
SANSOM STREET ENTRANCE

RAINGARDEN AREA FOR
STORMWATER COLLECTION
WITH NATIVE VEGETATION
AND BENCH SEATING

Building Consensus

The project was entirely collaborative, including input from parents, teachers, administrators, students, and partner organizations during both predesign and design development phases. The first step for volunteer architecture and engineering firm Kling Stubbins was to convene a community task force that included students, teachers, and parents from Greenfield as well as the Center City District, the Center City Residents' Association, the Philadelphia Water Department, and the Pennsylvania Horticultural Society.

Phasing into Green

Preliminary design was instrumental in getting the first major grant to hire a sustainable design team to develop the project. In 2009 and 2010, they added planting beds, shade trees, and rubberized play surfaces to the school yard. In spring 2011, the Greenfield HSA dedicated a "secret garden" that reclaimed what had been a dark, inaccessible, and underused corner of the grounds. Plans for the final phase are to install a green roof.

Everyone's involved: Greenfield students participated in the 2009 ribbon-cutting for phase one, which improved the western half of the play area.

Creating Gateways to the "The Ridge":
Roxborough Development Corporation

Animating the rise: "The Ridge" is a neighborhood artery that rises from the floodplain of the Schuylkill River at its east end to the radio towers that soar above Domino Lane at its west.

Ridge Avenue is an artery that covers five miles through the heart of Philadelphia's Roxborough section, and the design challenge here was to create gateways at either end. The Roxborough Development Corporation wanted to celebrate the avenue's central role, and to explore ideas for a public gathering space at its midpoint. The Collaborative's team designed a whimsical yet functional solution inspired by the local landscape and public art installations.

Location
Ridge Ave. at Osborne St. (east
end) and Domino Ln. (west
end), Roxborough neighborhood,
Philadelphia

Services completed
2006

Client
Roxborough Development
Corporation (RDC)

Volunteers
Tess Schiavone; Leslie Norvell;
Trevor Lee; Michael Funk

Hours donated (value)
169 ($15,810)

Products
Conceptual design

Built
No

A Leafy Solution for Two Extremes

The east end of Ridge Avenue, at Osborne Street, is narrow in scale as it rises sharply uphill, crowded by row houses and corner stores. The west end, at Domino Lane, has a diffuse series of parking lots, significant setbacks, and large utility poles. The design team adopted an ivy leaf motif and then adapted it to respond to the specific scale of the two gateway locations.

At the east end the team sought to convey a threshold, but at the west end, that same gateway structure would have been lost amid the other tall elements, so they transformed the leaf motif into a canopy overhanging bus shelters. Designs for Osborne Street were geared toward reinforcing the close-knit feel of this neighborhood, with street trees, sidewalk bump-outs, crosswalks, and urban pleasures like benches and a newsstand.

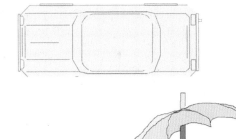

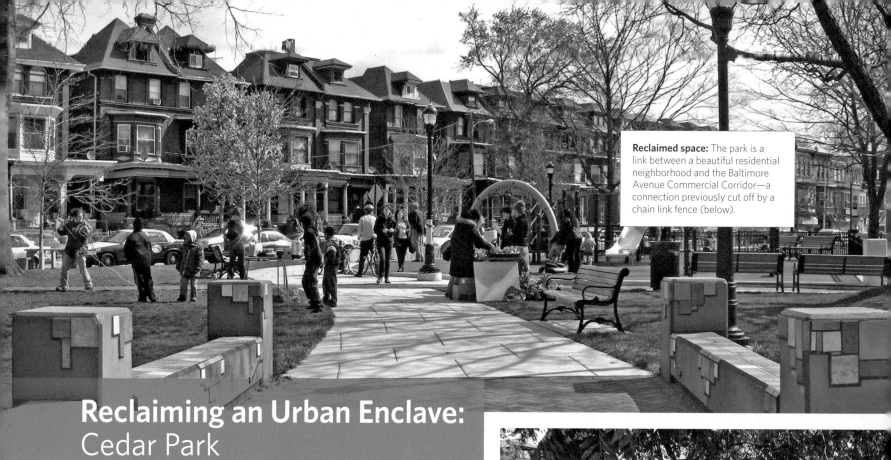

Reclaimed space: The park is a link between a beautiful residential neighborhood and the Baltimore Avenue Commercial Corridor—a connection previously cut off by a chain link fence (below).

Reclaiming an Urban Enclave:
Cedar Park

Location
4900 block of Baltimore Ave.
(at South 50th St.), Cedar Park
neighborhood, Philadelphia

Services completed
2004

Client
Cedar Park Neighbors
Community Association

Volunteers
Dan Garofalo, AIA; Anne
Harnish; Robert Lundgren;
Laura Raymond

Hours donated (value)
131 ($10,700)

Products
Existing conditions assessment,
conceptual landscape
plan, preliminary cost estimate

Consultant for final design
Lager Raabe Skafte Landscape
Architects

Built
2006

The *Philadelphia City Paper* described how this project transformed what had been a "killing field" and a "cage" into a place to garden at twilight— "something that, just two years ago in Cedar Park, would have been unthinkable."[1]

1. Bruce Schimmel, "Good Design, Better Community," *Philadelphia City Paper,* May 27, 2008.

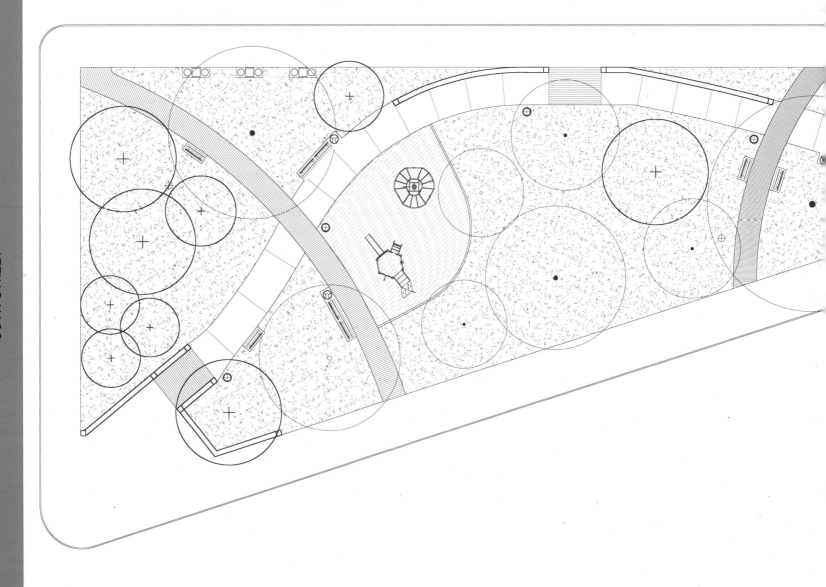

Community

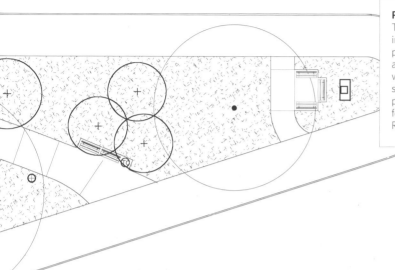

Preliminary to final:
The Collaborative redesigned interior paths to encourage pedestrian use, including seat walls and lighting for the paths at night, which increased visibility from the street. This preliminary landscape plan (right) provided the framework for the final design (left) by Lager Raabe Skafte Landscape Architects.

Taking Back the Park

Residents were eager to transform this triangular, half-acre public park near the University of Pennsylvania campus into a more attractive, safe, and engaging space that was integrated into the fabric of the neighborhood.

The site lies at the junction of a quiet residential street and the lively, pedestrian-friendly Baltimore Avenue Commercial Corridor, but the park had fallen into disrepair, and a chain link fence enclosing overgrown, hidden spaces made it a magnet for loitering, public drinking, and drug activity.

The preliminary design featured new pathways that opened up all the areas within the park and connected neighbors with Baltimore Avenue. The neighbors spearheaded other improvements including new playground equipment, tree plantings, a mosaic, and restoring the World War I memorial at the park's east end.

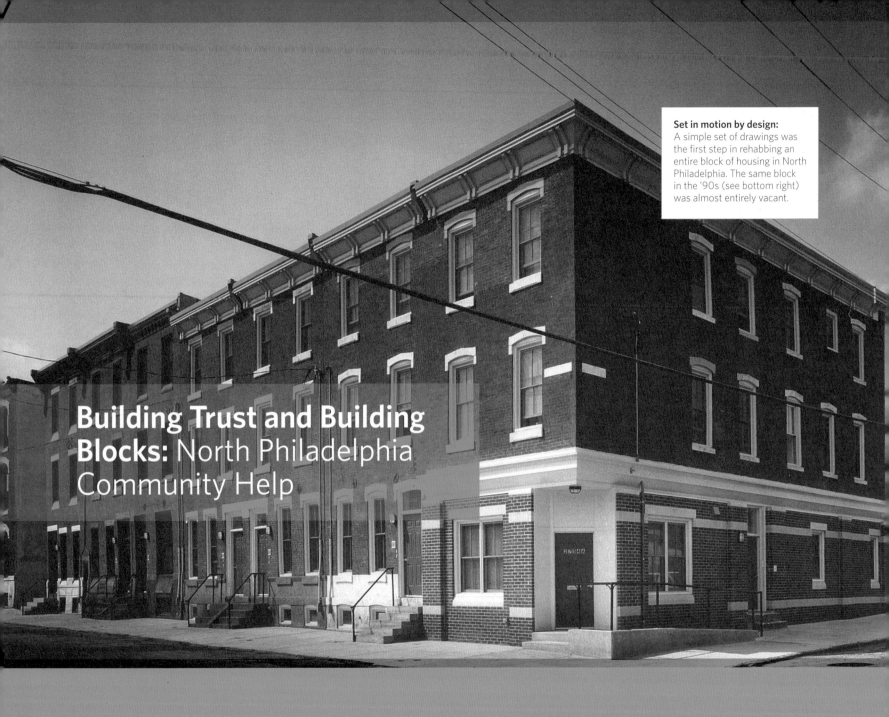

Set in motion by design:
A simple set of drawings was the first step in rehabbing an entire block of housing in North Philadelphia. The same block in the '90s (see bottom right) was almost entirely vacant.

Building Trust and Building Blocks: North Philadelphia Community Help

Community

Skip Biddle, director of North Philadelphia Community Help, became one of the Collaborative's first clients in 1991. He had acquired twenty abandoned row houses on North 11th Street, and his organization wanted to rehab them to rent to local residents. But he was faced with a dilemma: he couldn't get funding for the renovations without first documenting the project's scope and feasibility.

A Client's Chicken-Egg Dilemma

"Without funding," wrote Dan Garofalo in an early Collaborative newsletter, "[Skip] could not hire design professionals to begin any work at all." However, Skip was one of the community leaders in North Central Philadelphia to have forged relationships through AIA's Regional/Urban Design Action Team (R/UDAT) starting in 1990—a precursor to the Collaborative. So he reached out to Emanuel Kelly, AIA, to help him overcome that initial hurdle. Dan Garofalo and Mark Keener, two intern architects involved in the newly formed Collaborative, stepped up to help.

A Process at Work

Skip presented the Collaborative with photographs of the row houses, rough dimensions, and possible interiors, and Collaborative founders Dan and Mark created pen and ink drawings of initial layouts of all the houses. These went into a proposal that Skip presented to various funding agencies—with successful results.

He was able to secure funding from the U.S. Department of Housing and Urban Development, the Commonwealth of Pennsylvania Department of Community and Economic Development, and Philadelphia's Office of Housing and Community Development, as well as several private and foundation donors. The ribbon-cutting for the finished "Rose Garden Apartments" took place in 2000.

Location
2700 block of North 11th St. (at West Somerset St.), Hartranft neighborhood, Philadelphia

Services completed
1991

Client
North Philadelphia Community Help, Inc.

Volunteers
Dan Garofalo, AIA; Mark Keener, AIA

Hours donated (value)
15 ($1,200)

Products
Conceptual floor plans

Consultant for final design
Kelly/Maiello, Inc. Architects & Planners

Built
2000

Leverage: Strengthening Neighborhoods through Design

A 360° View, Part II: *The Power of Design*

Building Political Awareness

*Todd Woodward: The idea you've presented that "Everyone deserves good design" is a simple but important one. It seems to imply that "Everyone **appreciates** good design"— that it doesn't take a design education to appreciate a good public space. From your position now, what barriers do you see to achieving that? What prevents everyone from having the design they deserve?*

Alan Greenberger: Community Development Corporations (CDCs) and neighborhood groups should not shortchange their own right to decent design. It's not just the "haves" that do the shortchanging; sometimes the "have-nots" shortchange themselves, because they just don't believe it's theirs to have.

Beth Miller: When we're working primarily with nonprofit CDCs, design isn't high on their priority list, but in the context of finding solutions for other issues, when they see it as a tool that can add value, then they are willing to invest. And that's what we're trying to give them: that first couple of steps of getting other people to see that value, whether it be their board members—who don't necessarily see design as a line item on their budgets—or their City Council person.

So **it's about building political awareness (with a small "p")**, and how we build design advocacy in general. I see how organizations like the Mayors' Institute on City Design are trying to create this bigger political awareness, and trying to understand what role community design centers play in that constellation of activities. It takes all of them, but I'd like to hear your experience, Maurice, at the National Endowment for the Arts, and Alan, your experience in Philadelphia.

Alan: This idea that design creates value is an important premise. **People often forget—or are willing to discount—the power of design in their physical environment to create value.** With products, this power [of design] is [evident] all the time. For a lot of companies, design has saved their necks. Two noteworthy examples are the VW Beetle, or the iMac. Apple is thought of as the leading design company in the world of computers. Everyone who works in computers recognizes that it is high-quality design.

Todd: Working with nonprofits as our clients—either as a Collaborative volunteer, or as an architect in the private industry—[I see that] they don't want to put money into their facility; they want all of it to go to their mission. They don't realize that how they inhabit their own facility says a lot about their mission and could even enhance their mission.

Alan: At the same time, designers have to know when to step back.

Beth: No "Mighty Mouse" architecture. We're not here to save the day.

Maurice Cox: There is a challenge when you talk about good design of environments, versus design of products. People interface with gadgets every day and they know what amenities make them superior products. When it comes to environments, people intuitively know what a comfortable or acceptable environment looks and feels like: a pedestrian scale, things visually attract them as they walk down the street, sidewalks that are not obstacle courses, places that seem to be dominated by pedestrians over cars. All of that sounds like a downtown—more than their neighborhoods. **People place a lot of value in the quality of neighborhoods.** As goes the downtown, so goes the city, and (rightfully) a lot of cities focus on their downtowns. But if you can talk about quality of life in people's neighborhoods, you can grab them where they live.

Beth: On their front stoop.

Maurice: **Community design centers have been fostering the idea that if the heart of the city is the downtown, then the soul of a city is its neighborhoods.** You can look at what kinds of amenities people appreciate in their neighborhoods. When you talk about that, you are working where people live. Some of the stark contrasts in neighborhoods have to do with landscape and how mature it is, how stark. Whether you can get a good walk, whether it's tree-covered, decades old or centuries old, versus what you see in an impoverished neighborhood that is completely devoid of landscape.

An area of focus for the Collaborative is getting back to the quality of residential neighborhoods, small commercial centers, and little main streets—where people are inclined to go on a daily basis to do their shopping. If we engage people in conversations about where they live, I see them giving greater value to design quality.

And it might be a process of maturing, because this is not a conversation that is exclusive of downtowns. When you're dealing with downtown, you're dealing with a scale of development, with enormous economic interests, and very complex dynamics. With residential areas, it's a matter of blocks, residents, community facilities, walkability—all those things are synonymous with quality of life. It's a wonderful thing to have people talking about the places that they care about. I've found **it's easier to have a conversation about shared values—about quality of life, about design—when it's about a neighborhood.**

Tackling Problems as Designers

Todd: **How have your experiences as designers and as architects—both as educators and in practice—influenced your other roles, in government and elsewhere?**

Maurice: Part of the power of practicing is that you run smack into the regulatory process—what it enables, and what it doesn't. [Going through] the process of trying to get through a zoning ordinance—for a mixed-used building, for example, which you learn is illegal—is invaluable, in terms of seeing how rules dictate form.

I discovered that our commercial corridor couldn't support a mixed-use residential anchored corridor. So we came to a community vision; an idea might be a pedestrian-oriented midscale, mixing residential over retail. And then you go to regulatory enabling ordinances and learn that you can't produce that building. That's when you realize that **the rules have to be changed.** If you'd never gone through the process of trying to get the project to happen, you wouldn't have learned that there was a disconnect between the two.

Using practical experiences like that, or the issue of creating a vibrant main street corridor in a neighborhood, you find out you don't have residential density or the variety of housing types that would attract the cross section who would patronize those businesses. Then you have to look at: What are our residential densities here? Do we enable low-rise multifamily units within the context of a single-family

neighborhood? Or do we have a neighborhood of ten units an acre and never get to critical mass that could support downtown retail? The applications of practice yields where you need significant adaptation to let something transformative happen.

Alan: I like to use my discipline base to challenge lawyers. To the extent that the Collaborative is involved in some of that envisioning, this is where a planner with an economics background can be very helpful. This is a bunch of math: to look at the demographics of a place, densities of population, and to be able to say to people, "You all want a supermarket, but it's not going to happen here, because there are three already—here, here, and here—and you don't have the critical mass to make work a business that operates on incredibly tight margins—let alone to get it built."

Approaches to Infill Housing

Todd: **How has being an architect or designer influenced how you tackle housing problems?**

Maurice: I remember trying to create small opportunities for local contractors to do infill housing in the city [of Charlottesville, VA]. Much like Philadelphia, we had thousands— not tens of thousands—of nonconforming lots. We finally decided to do inventory of all vacant lots. Many had houses on them once, but when they were demolished, they were not being redeveloped and lay vacant, because now—due to the highly suburban zoning ordinances of the 1990s—they didn't meet the square feet requirements. So we removed that requirement, so you could build a house that would meet the street and replicate some of the massing that had happened once upon a time.

But if someone hadn't looked at the law and seen that there was a gap between the kind of housing we wanted to build and the regulation that did not allow it, we would not have been able to change that around. This allowed a whole new group of design-build projects—one or two at a time in traditional neighborhoods, with interesting experiments in contemporary design that you could find anywhere. It's important to know what you're trying to capture in terms of design excellence, and to look inevitably at the hurdles that design policy is putting before a particular project.

Alan: A developer who does infill housing—in a lot more of [Philadelphia] than you might realize—came to me recently and showed me a stack of what he's done: ones, twos, and fours. I cringed at the design of some of them, but others were getting better. This happens in neighborhoods that have bottomed out but, for one reason or another, the market has proven worthy: Kensington, Fishtown, Point Breeze.

Beth: These are "vital neighborhoods."

Alan: Some neighborhoods grudgingly go along, and some fight it tooth and nail because it looks like gentrification and they are disturbed by the changes that are coming. You can't solve that just by design. But to the extent that this developer is making his houses look and feel more responsive to the street, he ups the chance of it working, and creates a more pleasant and more agreeable experience for those who are sticking around.

In one instance, there's a bay window on the second or third floor and there's a painful difference between what the house communicated and what the developer communicated about what his intentions were in the neighborhood. I told this guy I'd help him try to cut through some of the regulatory front, but also said, "If you're going to do this sort of stuff, you've got to obligate yourself to do better work with better firms." I showed him where he was doing it better, and where he wasn't, and he got it. Will he do it [right] every time? No.

Maurice: Here's where the Collaborative can be so valuable: **there are great examples of design-build—young firms that are willing to take a risk to develop areas of Philadelphia that haven't seen innovation in a very long time.** Onion Flats[1] is a classic example of [a firm] going into neighborhoods and doing high-quality work. There are enormous numbers of young entrepreneurs who are willing to do this. That's what I loved about being in city government; I would see this and say, "Let's hold a focus group and figure out how to do more of this."

They were the ones who would say: "The lots we like to build on are all nonconforming, so if you did this, or that, we could do a lot more infill housing." That kind of **entrepreneurial reflection is something the Collaborative can easily do for a city**, whereas City Hall not so much.

Beth: One of my favorite examples, which has yet to be built, was on our first Infill pilot on affordable housing. Tim McDonald of Onion Flats was on a jury and made a suggestion to one of the teams. They implemented it, and it was a much better product at the end of the day. But the product that did get developed was with Asociación Puertorriqueños en Marcha (APM), a very high-capacity CDC. It was a back-burner project; someone had suggested some green housing from a class at the University of Pennsylvania. A young firm, Interface Studio, tried it and came up with a scheme for affordable green housing now called Sheridan Street. It's been built and received PHFA[2] funding. This provides a different product for that community and was an impetus for the 100K house by Postgreen[3], so it's actually spun off in these other directions in the private sector. It's rare that **this kind of trickle-up theory works**, but it did in this instance.

Design versus Implementation

Todd: **What's the biggest challenge in bringing projects to fruition?**

Alan: The biggest barrier to achieving good design is ultimately the decision tree that tries to weigh all of the issues in front of place-making. Design is one of them, but so are economics, political will, and the organizational ability of the sponsor of the project. **You have to get all the stars to align to make something happen.**

In my new role[4] I'm discovering the challenge of getting to the point where projects actually exist and people agree that they know how to do it and have an idea of how to pay for it. This is extremely hard—particularly in a difficult economic environment. And it is not solely a question of where the money is, although that's a big part of it. It's also a question of who is the sponsor, where is the willpower, who has organized a community's general support and participation, who is assuming the ongoing maintenance costs, and who is assuming the liabilities in an ongoing way. These are huge issues, and typically they don't have natural answers.

One of the criticisms leveled at design is that good design is relatively easy to envision, and almost impossible to implement—**the implementation is where the real heroics are.** There's a fair amount of truth to that. However, it's not fair to separate quality design, as if it exists solely as a series of ideas on paper.

Ultimately, **quality design manifests itself through the implementation process,** and ideally it survives the implementation process, so that what you get in the end is actually a good thing, with a method to care for it. That takes a lot of hard work, because it requires people to step back from an idealized design future and make compromises.

Actually **I see it as a more dynamic, integrated process, in which good design emerges in the context of an implementation strategy.** And that's a reality, by itself. Architects, planners, and designers tend to see it as compromise of a vision, and there are times when it is. But the weakness of that statement is the premise going in—that idealized design absent implementation…has an essential truth to it, and if it can't [be implemented], then it doesn't have that essential truth. Idealized design is just that. It's aspirational; it's a wish list.

People shouldn't think [of it as] compromising; they should see it as refining and perfecting [the product]—getting to the point where they can live with it and experience the benefit that comes from it. It's about what the Collaborative and AIA and the Design Advocacy Group have been saying forever: **Design needs to be on the table.** If it's not on the table, it will get cut, because money generally will win out.

If it's on the table, it gets perfected and refined and made into what it can and should be—possibly not to everyone's liking. You win some and you lose some, [but] winning some and losing some in the big city is okay. It's like the baseball season: 162 games, and no one wins much more than 100. You don't go out and win every time.

Beth: I like what you said about how good design emerges as part of an implementation strategy. That's a part of what the Collaborative pushes for: that design is part of a process to improve neighborhoods and strengthen them. Good design without implementation, is it really good design? How do you make it work in reality?

Alan: It may be good theoretical design.

Beth: But we want to be pragmatic.

Alan: There's nothing wrong with theory, with being aspirational. There's nothing wrong with showing people the best you have to offer. But people should take it for what it's worth: it's idealized, a vision without the means to realize it. Yet. Obviously this varies with the sponsors and what financial position they are in to [realize a project].

At the level of planning—and [I know] the Collaborative engages in a great deal of planning, both at the architectural level and mini urban scale—**one of the [objectives] is to put a set of ideas in people's heads.** This is part of the process of building a collective will, [to help them realize]: "This is important; I can kind of taste it. Some folks have shown us how it might pan out, and this is what we want."

In a world that's like going to a supermarket—a tidal wave of possibility, too many choices, possibilities, things to get done—and you can't get them all done, so you have to pick. The way you pick is by picking winners, **[a project] where there is some collective will to do something. Those are the ones that get done.** Anyone interested in getting things done wants to gravitate to that. Planning is a way to organize will—and ultimately money—to implement projects, based on a premise of how people might live better.

1 An architecture/development firm in Philadelphia. www.onionflats.com

2 Philadelphia Housing Finance Agency.

3 See http://postgreen.com and http://hybridconstruct.com

4 Mr. Greenberger is Deputy Mayor for Commerce and Economic Development and Executive Director of the Philadelphia City Planning Commission.

When Is Collaboration Like Construction?

BY MARK ALAN HUGHES

A FEW YEARS AGO, I was struck that a famous architect began a lecture at Carpenters' Hall in Philadelphia with the claim: "I do not build, because I am an architect." The key to keeping that manifesto from slipping into effete, elite nonsense is to couple it, when possible, with an authentic readiness to build. That creative tension—between demanding design and satisfactory structure—has been the sweet space the Community Design Collaborative has occupied for twenty years. At its best, ready-to-build collaboration creates so much value that construction can be either the icing or the cake; it really doesn't matter.

I am grateful for the chance to celebrate the twentieth anniversary by raising three issues provoked by the past and future of the Collaborative. First, software companies speak of "fragmentation" as one consequence of rapid innovation. For example, there are four or five versions of Google's relatively new and rapidly evolving Android operating system in use, making it difficult for other actors (e.g., consumers, app designers) to find a stable platform on which to learn, invest, and operate. I adopt this concept of fragmentation to consider the many productive organizations now at work on community design in Philadelphia. That is, in this case, fragmentation is not a bad thing; rather, it is a consequence of a good thing: rapid innovation within this issue network. So the challenge for funders and policymakers is how to embrace fragmentation that results from the balancing of innovation and stability. And the challenge for innovators like the Collaborative is how to survive fragmentation and embody the stability that funders and decision makers characteristically seek, without losing the spirit of innovation.

Secondly, this anniversary inspires thoughts about transformation. What is the Collaborative's endgame? Any creatively disruptive activity and (especially) organization provokes this question. Fragmentation, is about what's going on "outside" among all the related design organizations. Transformation is about what's going on between the "outside" and the "inside." Will the Collaborative's ultimate success be eventually to transform the "inside" so that the organization itself goes out of business? Think of LEED and other third-party certifications of green buildings. If their highest standards all became mandatory code, would they feel they had accomplished their mission and close up shop? A challenge for any organization facing a twentieth anniversary is determining whether to transform the status quo in a way that makes it obsolete or to create a permanent future for itself and the need it fills.

Beyond fragmentation and transformation, I suggest a reconciliation: an appraisal of the Collaborative's work and role that reconciles the tensions I have introduced here. This reconciliation returns to the idea that good collaboration is just as valuable as good construction.

Other contributors to this volume have traced the history of the Collaborative and the generations of related work traceable to the 1970s. In Philadelphia, the current generation (third? Y? millennial?) consists of such rich varieties that networks are almost as prevalent as organizations: we have the support of the Design Advocacy Group of Philadelphia (DAG), Penn Praxis, PlanPhilly, Design Philadelphia, the Center for Architecture, the Central Delaware Advocacy Group, Next Great City, and the Built Environment Coalition, to name a few. The Philadelphia mayoral election of 2007 helped foster a perfect storm for this cluster of issues, especially with the Next Great City coalition. Mayor Michael A. Nutter has often noted that Next Great City sponsored the first of 40 mayoral forums and that his study of and commitment to their ten-point platform launched the momentum that carried him into office. Nutter's repeated promise and continuing efforts to restore the authority of planning and design in the City have probably encouraged and certainly cultivated this innovation and, as defined above, fragmentation.

These efforts share a commitment to making an intentional choice of an alternative future that is empowered by a technical expertise. This approach shares much with policy strategy, and so these efforts helped create the conditions under which the Mayor's Office of Sustainability could create and enact a policy strategy like Greenworks

Philadelphia,[1] even though its substance is technically quite different from the typical Collaborative project. The common ground lies in the attempt to make responsible choices in the present to improve outcomes in the future. That approach may be so fundamental to design thinking that designers may underappreciate its impact on the general public. But it is hard to imagine a mayor moving community expectations from the transactional mode of the 1990s and early 2000s to the visionary mode of Greenworks, the Civic Vision for the Central Delaware,[2] and Philadelphia2035[3] without the cultivation of design thinking by the Collaborative, DAG, and others.

Out in those vineyards, the Collaborative has labored to demonstrate these possible alternative futures in neighborhoods and among communities that might otherwise have been thought too stressed, too poor, too ethnic—too whatever—to move beyond transactions for transactions' sake. Stress can indeed drain the resources needed to make an intentional choice from among alternative futures that have been empowered by expertise. For twenty years, the Collaborative has helped fill funding and policy gaps by creating design clients among organizations in places that might otherwise would not have been able—as we say in sustainability: to "pay the first costs for design," and it ended up suffering the far greater lifecycle costs for bad design. By fostering such a clientele, the Collaborative has overcome more than just a lack of resources. Often, communities without sufficient resources are also communities low on the list of priorities for decision makers, whether public or private. Giving voice to those further down the list can help change the priorities themselves, providing benefits far beyond the boundaries of a single improved project

I suggested that fragmentation is a complicating consequence of lively innovation, as Philadelphia has witnessed in design in the past few years. Foundations and others have observed that, as choices proliferate, funders and decision makers face so many options that the sheer number of potential grantees, advisers, and worthy causes no longer seems to bring order to the world. One solution to fragmentation is consolidation, in which the strongest features of previous versions are all gathered in a single (presumably, but not always, the latest) version. Another solution is confederation, in which the collaborators network their strengths. These are solutions for those who need to balance innovation with stability, like funders or decision makers, but for the innovators themselves, fragmentation is about the need to stand out in a crowd, and neither consolidation nor confederation necessarily makes that easier.

The Collaborative's twenty years of practice immunize it from the risks (to innovators) of either consolidation or confederation. Who else combines the advantages of being disciplined by the realities of single projects with the advantages of being about different projects every year? Who else speaks to the most powerful elements of Philadelphia's design and policy community while always making a place in that conversation for those otherwise absent? Who else brings the most politically scalable element— ordinary people and their advocates—into the process of designing better buildings under real conditions? The best way to respond to fragmentation is to make yourself indispensible.

Mayor Nutter's repeated promise and continuing efforts to restore the authority of planning and design in the City have probably encouraged and certainly cultivated this innovation.

Brilliant ideas are often conceived as second-best solutions. In fact, it is usually easier to dream up the kind of textbook or first-best solutions that require a "magic wand" of assumptions and "if-only"s than it is to devise solutions that accept certain realities and work around them. Good design, especially as it creates outcomes with increased site or neighborhood benefits or more efficient use of resources, is a compelling public interest that warrants resources and regulation. And this is especially true when the ability to pay means that access to good design is unevenly distributed in Philadelphia—and everywhere else. But, for the foreseeable future, that first-best solution of public processes capable of ensuring good design in every project requires a magic wand, and certainly did twenty years ago.

We needed then—and need today—the Community Design Collaborative. What does it mean that we still need it twenty years later? Would we want a world that didn't need it? How does the answer to that question affect what the Collaborative does? These questions confront an organization that is in the position to continue to transform the world it finds. Two decades has meant 600 projects—more than enough to ask whether the Collaborative has changed the game. My answer is yes, but maybe the Collaborative hasn't changed the game you think.

The new Greater Philadelphia Innovation Cluster (GPIC) at the Navy Yard, funded by the Department of Energy, has a fairly specific theory of change. The idea is that existing technologies are largely capable of achieving huge increases in the energy efficiency of buildings, but these technologies face a number of obstacles that prevent them from being widely adopted in the regional marketplace. So GPIC is designed to demonstrate and deploy energy efficiency in buildings using partnerships, information, training, financing, and regulations that support technology in the market. The theory is that, with enough demonstration and deployment, the market will accept and widely adopt increased energy efficiency in this region and beyond. This is a model that plans for GPIC to go out of business because of the transformation it effects.

We could think of the Collaborative as playing a similar role: teaching the city and region about the advantages of good design until the lesson catches on and the Collaborative is no longer needed. And some of that is probably happening. Collaborative partners who "discover" the returns to good design might go on to build resources for it in future projects. Neighbors of Collaborative projects who have observed that value of good design might seek it out when they consider building. In fact, the Collaborative's role is different than GPIC, with a different connection between the "outside" and

When Is Collaboration Like Construction?

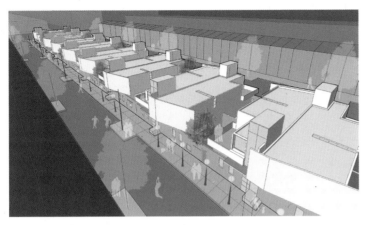

the "inside." The Collaborative isn't only about leveraging enlightened self-interest in order to produce more well-designed projects. The Collaborative is also about the considerably more ambitious work of collective action. No amount of deployment will ever ensure that private development alone will create enough design value in the commons shared by all who benefit from good design. And no amount of demonstration will ever ensure that every community can afford to pay for good design, even when every community wants it.

In other words, the Collaborative isn't just trying to create clients for good design, because even if everyone in Philadelphia had been part of a Collaborative project it still wouldn't be enough to transform the status quo. The real game the Collaborative is changing is in trying to create constituents for good design. And it is not a game where the outside can get elected to reform the inside and then go home. As Lincoln Steffens noted a little over a hundred years ago, Philadelphians have a fondness for reform because they have such a distaste for governing. They want to fix things and go home. But the real challenge is continuous good governance. And on our issues, that takes a permanent constituency for good design. For large parts of Philadelphia, it is hard to imagine sustaining that constituency without the Collaborative.

So both fragmentation and transformation argue that we need at least another twenty years of the Collaborative. So how do we reconcile all that complexity, significance, and ambition with the demands of sustaining a small nonprofit organization? What's the right metric for the Collaborative? What's the basis for outsiders supporting its future?

The key to these questions may in fact come from the idea of leverage,

which is the advantage deriving from position to act effectively. It seems to me that the yield of the Collaborative isn't the number of projects that actually get constructed, or even the value of the donated design services. The yield is the impact that comes from all the collaborations it has and will convene, all the parties to those collaborations, all the projects ever done by those parties, and all the observers of those collaborations, whether they be competitors or colleagues, active participants or interested bystanders. Now that's leverage! Each of those gears turns other gears and generates impact. When those collaborations are done well and include those who would otherwise miss out, they create the constituencies for good design.

Only the Community Design Collaborative has the leverage—the position to act effectively—to create and sustain these constituencies among much of the City. The Collaborative's legacy shows that collaboration can be as good as construction, when that collaboration is disciplined by an authentic readiness to build, if possible. This story is one worth talking about at Carpenters' Hall.

1 In 2009 Mayor Nutter's Office of Sustainability created Greenworks Philadelphia, an ambitious plan that targets fifteen sustainability issues in energy, environment, equity, economy, and engagement, as part of an effort to make Philadelphia the greenest city in America by 2015. http://www.phila.gov/green/greenworks

2 A year of intense civic engagement and thinking about the future of the Delaware Riverfront resulted in this 2007 report, by Penn Praxis at the School of Design at UPenn, the Penn Project on Civic Engagement, the Philadelphia City Planning Commission. http://planphilly.com/vision

3 Managed by the Philadelphia City Planning Commission starting in 2010, this is the city's first comprehensive strategic plan in 50 years. http://phila2035.org

DESIGN

The Collaborative's volunteers are all designers, of one kind or another, and all want to use their skills to improve our city. The Collaborative strives to provide design expertise to underserved neighborhoods at a level of quality that was previously unprecedented for community design projects. Many of the projects over the last twenty years exemplify design excellence and represent thoughtful and beautiful expressions of civic design.

Selective Subtraction:
Oxford Street

Inspiring and functional: With this project, the Collaborative explored combining industrial uses with housing at an under-utilized site. At the entrance to the courtyard would be an industrial garden, which DIGSAU architect Jules Dingle described as "a gorgeous landscape where you can see people doing manufacturing work."

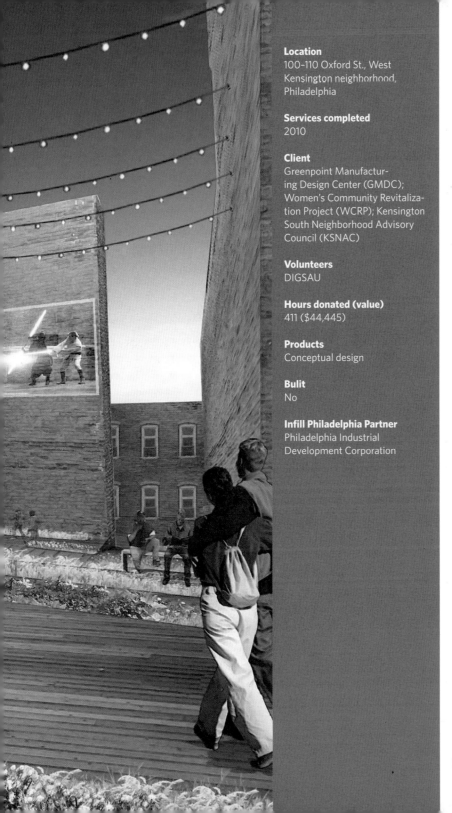

Location
100-110 Oxford St., West
Kensington neighborhood,
Philadelphia

Services completed
2010

Client
Greenpoint Manufactur-
ing Design Center (GMDC);
Women's Community Revitaliza-
tion Project (WCRP); Kensington
South Neighborhood Advisory
Council (KSNAC)

Volunteers
DIGSAU

Hours donated (value)
411 ($44,445)

Products
Conceptual design

Bulit
No

Infill Philadelphia Partner
Philadelphia Industrial
Development Corporation

The challenge here was to reuse a site that was essentially a crowded old factory complex in a neighborhood of row houses that were interspersed with factories and workshops. A "fine-tuned demolition" opened up all sorts of possibilities, including a mixed-use community that combines 34 units of affordable housing and 45 studios of artisan workspace, as well as a landscaped ramp leading from an "industrial garden" at ground level to the rooftop garden for residents.

Carving Out a Courtyard

Through what they termed "selective subtraction," the architects shaved away eight percent of the factory structures. While the current site's six disparate buildings (see below) are clustered close together, the design carved out space for a courtyard to bring natural light into building interiors and create a landscaped ramp that spirals up through the courtyard, connecting floors, studios, and housing. The design uses the character of the existing buildings and site to create a progression of views and spatial experiences.

A Philly/New York Partnership
This development project with WCRP was one of the first in Philadelphia for New York–based GMDC, which has rehabilitated several Brooklyn manufacturing buildings for occupancy by small manufacturers, artisans, and artists. The two community development organizations share a mission of creating affordable housing and jobs within a community.

Filling in: Oxford Street was one of several old industrial sites the Collaborative targeted for an initiative called Infill Philadelphia, created to help urban communities rethink the use of older spaces and re-envision their neighborhoods.

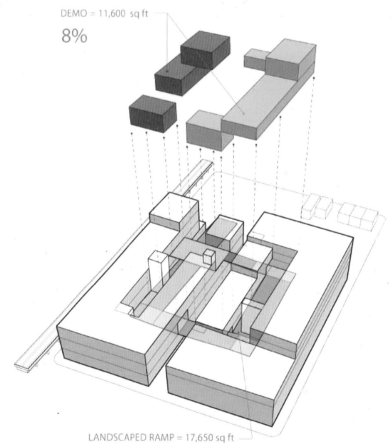

DEMO = 11,600 sq ft

8%

LANDSCAPED RAMP = 17,650 sq ft

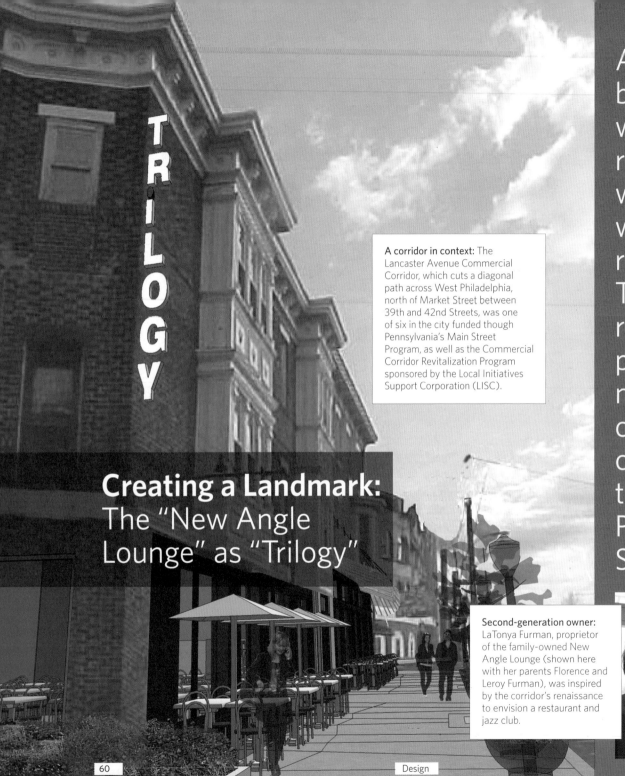

A family-owned business that was ripe for reinvention was paired with a fluid but respectful design. The results reflected renewed prospects for neighborhood commercial corridors like this one in West Philadelphia's Saunders Park.

A corridor in context: The Lancaster Avenue Commercial Corridor, which cuts a diagonal path across West Philadelphia, north of Market Street between 39th and 42nd Streets, was one of six in the city funded though Pennsylvania's Main Street Program, as well as the Commercial Corridor Revitalization Program sponsored by the Local Initiatives Support Corporation (LISC).

Creating a Landmark:
The "New Angle Lounge" as "Trilogy"

Second-generation owner: LaTonya Furman, proprietor of the family-owned New Angle Lounge (shown here with her parents Florence and Leroy Furman), was inspired by the corridor's renaissance to envision a restaurant and jazz club.

Design

A Commercial Infill

The New Angle Lounge—a neighborhood pub—was one of several commercial corridor sites designers reconceived through the Collaborative's Infill Philadelphia initiative, created to help urban communities proactively rethink the use of older spaces, in order to re-envision their neighborhoods.

People's Emergency Center (PEC), a community development and social services agency based nearby, thought the New Angle Lounge and its owner, LaTonya Furman, would be a good match for Infill Philadelphia. The new design presents the building as a lively, engaging gateway to the Lancaster Avenue commercial corridor.

Designing a New Angle

The predesign approach combined the first floors of three adjacent buildings to create a larger, more flexible floor plate that was large enough to accommodate a full-service restaurant—an amenity that is rare but extremely desirable on developing commercial corridors like this one. The triangular site was the inspiration for "Trilogy," a combined jazz club and restaurant that would populate the space during the day and into the evening.

The design team sought to take advantage of the flexibility afforded by the first-floor space, which—unlike the other floors—had already been modernized but was almost completely sealed up. Predesign devised a strategy to reanimate this space with large windows opening onto the sidewalk.

The challenge was to make these elements work together with preservation efforts on the upper floors, given the need to respect the historic urban fabric of Lancaster Avenue. The solution was a sculptural canopy that would wrap around the building, providing cover for outside seating, while contrasting the finely detailed bays and cornices that would be restored on the building's upper stories.

Opening up options: The design creates vitality at night, with large first-floor windows that allow for activity and light from the restaurant, club, and lounge to spill out onto Lancaster Avenue. The same windows provide ample natural light for lunchtime patrons.

Location
3901–05 Lancaster Ave. (at 39th and Spring Garden Sts.), West Powelton/Saunders Park neighborhoods, Philadelphia

Services completed
2007

Client
People's Emergency Center (PEC)

Volunteers
CICADA Architecture/Planning, Inc.

Hours donated (value)
258 ($27,020)

Products
Conceptual design

Features
Contemporary facade and canopy on first floor, preservation of original building elements on upper floors

Built
No

Infill Philadelphia Partner
LISC Philadelphia

School as Beacon:
Byron Story Foundation

Juanita Story-Jones is a shining example of a Collaborative client who is passionately absorbed by a mission of service, but also attuned to the power of symbols—and of architecture—for a community. Moving the foundation she'd started in her son's honor into a newly designed space struck her as a chance to transform her vision for this alternative school into (literally) a "beacon of light" for the neighborhood. The Collaborative was more than happy to help.

Design

Facade that tells a story:
The facade design features a sidewalk-to-roof image of Byron Story's graduation portrait, created out of 450 translucent 4-inch snapshots of BSF students. The composite image speaks poetically to the collective benefit that has emerged from Byron Story's tragic death. The remainder of the facade is a translucent glass channel, and the light that filters through at night creates the beacon of light that Ms. Story-Jones envisioned.

Location
1646 Ridge Ave. (off Broad
St.), Francisville neighborhood,
Philadelphia

Services completed
2007

Client
Byron Story Foundation (BSF)

Volunteers
bwa architecture + planning;
International Consultants, Inc.

Hours donated (value)
215 ($21,125)

Built
No

"The building's
architectural expression
was inspired by a simple
question: 'If this building
were a store, what would
it be selling?' The answer
came back almost
immediately: 'Hope'."
—*Bill Becker, AIA, leader of
volunteer design team*

[byron story foundation]

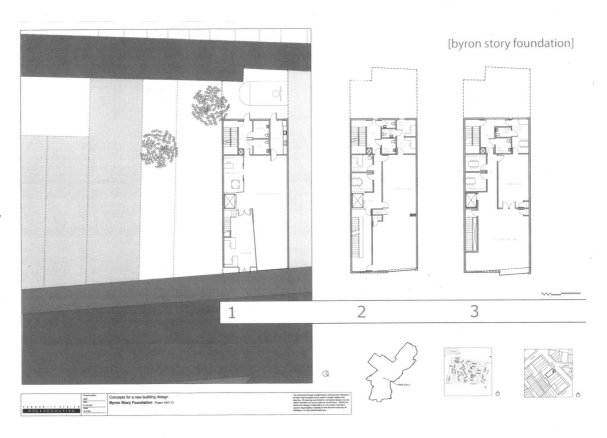

Honoring a Legacy

In the wake of losing her son Byron to handgun violence in 2002, Ms. Story-Jones decided to honor his memory in an exceptional way: by reaching out to help the young people who were most at risk for falling victim to (and perpetrating) this same violence. Soon after, she created the Byron Story Foundation (BSF), an alternative education center that provides "wraparound" services to at-risk youth, through a contract with the School District of Philadelphia.

Four years later, BSF staff struggled to do justice to its ambitious list of activities—teaching, tutoring, counseling, and special events—within the 1,700-foot space on the first floor of an aging Francisville row house. When a larger vacant space became available on the same block, the foundation saw an opportunity to expand in order to offer more services to more young people.

Manifesting a Mother's Vision

Juanita Story-Jones is not only an exceptional person—given her determination and commitment to helping kids who had been truant or dropped out of the public school system. She also had a unique ability to interpret her vision through collaboration with the design team. The dramatic and contemporary result was a design that successfully interpreted Ms. Story-Jones's goal for the building, including a fascinating yet approachable facade.

A personal investment: "Every project has a story; but this one really hit home. Juanita Story-Jones (above) stood up, took charge, and said 'This isn't going to happen anymore on my watch'."
—*Jessica Brams-Miller, a design team member*

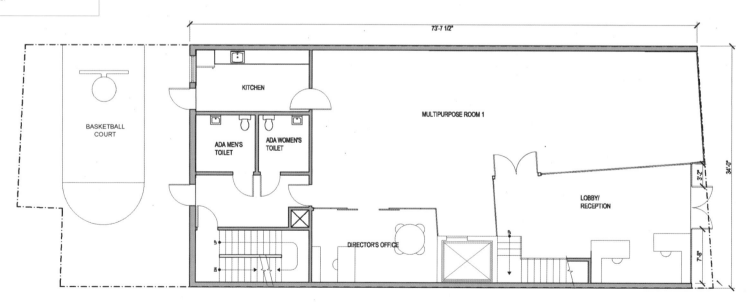

Pushing the Envelope:
APM's Affordable Infill Housing at Sheridan Street

Over the past decade, the community design corporation Asociación Puertorriqueños en Marcha (APM) has created hundreds of affordable housing units in its neighborhood, on the fringes of Temple University to the west, and Northern Liberties to the south. In 2005 they sought to diversify how they developed housing in this transforming area and brought the Collaborative on board.

Mix and match: Individual units can be customized by swapping living and sleeping spaces, creating two-story loft spaces, or converting an upper bedroom into a terrace, but none of these would affect the building footprint.

Design

Location
1800 block of North Sheridan St. and 600 block of Berks St. (at North 7th St.), North Philadelphia

Services completed
2006

Client
Asociación Puertorriqueños en Marcha (APM)

Volunteers
Interface Studio

Hours donated (value)
197 ($21,400)

Products
Conceptual design

Sustainable design features
Environmentally sustainable building materials, customization to maximize benefits of each unit's solar exposures

Awards
2006 AIA Philadelphia Silver Award

Consultant for final design
Interface Studio Architects, LLC

Built
Under construction as of June 2011

Infill Philadelphia Partner (pilot program)
NeighborhoodsNow

Modern options: Pradera I and II are twin homes, and APM wanted to offer residents a sustainable option for affordable housing, while also creating a more contemporary vibe and a building that fit the modest site.

What Philadelphia does well:
The concept of the Sheridan Street design prototype garnered national attention and a partnership with Postgreen that led to inexpensive houses suited to row house neighborhoods.

Design

Creative Challenge

The project—one of three focused on affordable infill housing for older urban neighborhoods—was part of a larger initiative by NeighborhoodsNow on how to address obsolete housing and block configurations. The goal was to come up with new home and street design prototypes that fit in, but offered something new.

To encourage innovative solutions and spur a conversation between design experts and leaders in community development, the Collaborative sponsored the Design Challenge, in which three design teams developed and presented to a jury options for affordable infill housing that reflected each neighborhood's unique context, site, and market.

The three design "problems" posed through a Design Challenge led to three innovative approaches to affordable housing, to serve as models for neighborhoods facing similar scenarios. Most important, the results were exciting designs that organizations like APM could achieve within the parameters of affordable housing, and offered a number of sustainable elements.

Breakthroughs at Berks and Sheridan

The project encompassed one strip of vacant land on Sheridan Street and another small parcel around the corner on Berks Street. Sheridan Street presented a particular design challenge because it was only 40 feet deep—too narrow for conventional housing redevelopment—and wedged behind Pradera, new twin homes with yards that APM developed recently.

The design team created a relatively simple prototype that was based loosely on the dimensions of the typical Philadelphia row house (roughly 16' x 40'), but emphasized daylight and flexibility—and offered the possibility of prefabricated construction. A palette of environmentally friendly materials was used on each facade relative to its solar exposure and interior layout.

> "This design challenge shows that infill housing design in Philadelphia needs to be approached in a more serious way, and it can be."
> —*Lisa Armstrong, juror*

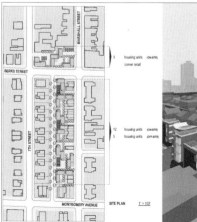

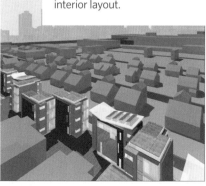

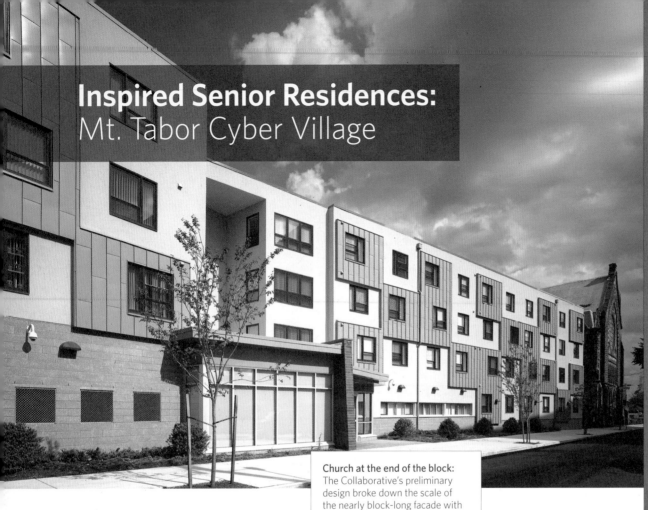

Inspired Senior Residences:
Mt. Tabor Cyber Village

Church at the end of the block:
The Collaborative's preliminary
design broke down the scale of
the nearly block-long facade with
an entrance at midblock, window
bays, and varied building materials.

Location
973 North 7th St. (at Poplar
St.), East Poplar neighborhood,
Philadelphia

Services completed
2005

Client
Mt. Tabor Community Educa-
tion and Economic Development
Corporation (Mt. Tabor CEED)

Volunteers
bwa architecture + planning;
Construction Management
Solutions; Thornton-Tomasetti

Hours donated (value)
430 ($39,516)

Products
Feasibility study and
conceptual design

Sustainable design features
Green roof

Consultant for final design
bwa architecture + planning

Built
2009

Design

Back in 2004, when Mt. Tabor Community Education and Economic Development Corporation (CEED) approached the Collaborative for conceptual design services, an urban Cyber Village for seniors was a cutting-edge concept. Reverends Mary Lou Moore and Martha Lang had worked for five years to acquire the vacant lot adjacent to Mt. Tabor African Methodist Episcopal (AME) Church, and they then fought to gain control of the lot from drug dealers and prostitutes. The ministers had a vision for a colorful, tech-savvy, and engaged senior community, but they needed the Collaborative to make a giant leap forward.

Inspired leadership: Reverends Mary Lou Moore and Martha Lang, leaders of Mt. Tabor CEED, are model clients with a passionate vision for change. "Existing senior facilities are depressing... The Lord placed it in my spirit to make a happy place to live."
—Rev. Lang

Envisioning Possibilities

Inspired by the ministers' passion and tenacity, the Collaborative did preliminary design work to prove that Mt. Tabor CEED could build enough units on the lot to make the project feasible. The design team also showed how the senior housing complex could feel welcoming, blend into the neighborhood, and serve a new generation of actively engaged seniors.

The conceptual design for the multi-story building consisted of two residential wings, joined by common rooms and a lobby at the main entrance. Much of the first floor—the café, computer center, fitness center, and community room—is also available for neighborhood use. Upstairs, lounges on each floor draw residents together, and outdoor gathering spaces and a greenway link the Cyber Village to Mt. Tabor AME Church and adjacent streets.

Creating Success

The strong preliminary design enabled Mt. Tabor CEED to maintain the integrity of its vision, despite a tight project timeline and budget. Mt. Tabor CEED hired bwa architecture + planning to join the development team, develop the project further, and apply for funding. They ultimately obtained affordable housing tax credits, and residents moved into the new space in 2009.

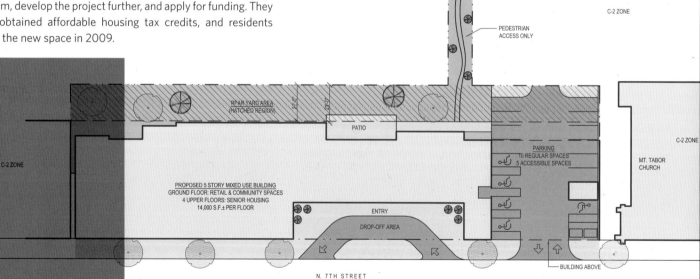

N. MARSHALL STREET

C-2 ZONE

PEDESTRIAN
ACCESS ONLY

REAR YARD AREA
(HATCHED REGION)

PATIO

PARKING
10 REGULAR SPACES
5 ACCESSIBLE SPACES

C-2 ZONE

MT. TABOR
CHURCH

C-2 ZONE

PROPOSED 5 STORY MIXED USE BUILDING
GROUND FLOOR: RETAIL & COMMUNITY SPACES
4 UPPER FLOORS: SENIOR HOUSING
14,000 S.F.± PER FLOOR

ENTRY

DROP-OFF AREA

BUILDING ABOVE

N. 7TH STREET

Design

"Mt. Tabor asked us from the beginning of the project to really work on developing community—in the neighborhood, with the church, and for the residents."
—*Brian Szymanik, AIA*

A gracious welcome: Mt. Tabor Cyber Village has a first-floor community room large enough for the entire population to gather, an outdoor patio, a community garden, and a 14,000-square-foot green roof—all of which inspire this diverse, thriving community to come together in new ways.

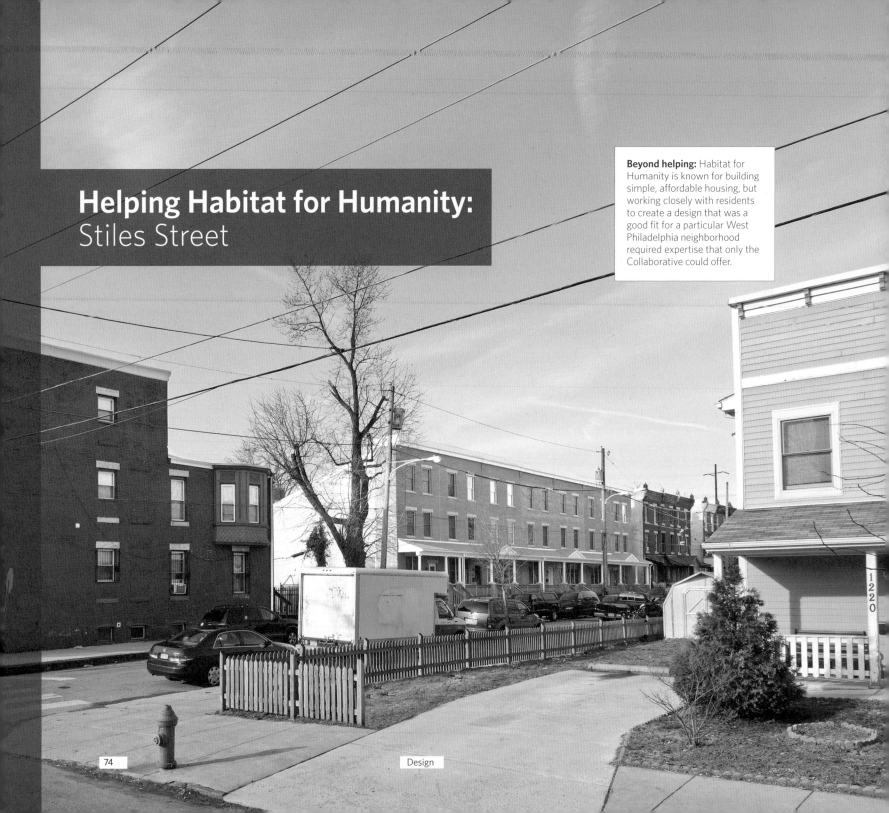

Helping Habitat for Humanity:
Stiles Street

Beyond helping: Habitat for Humanity is known for building simple, affordable housing, but working closely with residents to create a design that was a good fit for a particular West Philadelphia neighborhood required expertise that only the Collaborative could offer.

Design

Location
42nd and Stiles Sts., East
Parkside neighborhood,
West Philadelphia

Services completed
2006

Client
Habitat for Humanity
Philadelphia

Volunteer
Wallace Roberts & Todd (WRT);
Energy Coordinating Agency of
Philadelphia, Inc. (ECA)

Hours donated (value)
222 ($21,680)

Products
Conceptual block and site plans

Consultant for final design
Wallace Roberts & Todd (WRT)

Built
2009

When Habitat for Humanity approached the Collaborative about developing green affordable housing for a vacant lot in this East Parkside neighborhood, design aesthetics were the issue, and skilled community engagement was the solution.

Bridging Gaps, Facilitating Relationships

This East Parkside neighborhood had been disappointed with the results of two affordable housing units Habitat had constructed there in 2002, given that they did not suit the historic character of the neighborhood. So the humanitarian organization reached out to the Collaborative for help in building consensus for their next set of houses there. The Collaborative facilitated dialogue with the East Parkside Residents Association (EPRA) to get their feedback on—and buy-in for—the design options this time around.

Finding an Attractive Compromise

Habitat generally relies on simple designs that its volunteer construction crews can build easily. With this new housing, the organization needed to go beyond their standard unit—two-story frame twin homes with aluminum siding and sloped roofs—and devise a solution that integrated feedback from the community as well as practical building considerations.

Assembling a Green Team

The firm of Wallace Roberts & Todd (WRT) recruited volunteers from its staff and teamed up with the Philadelphia nonprofit Energy Coordinating Agency (ECA) to incorporate sustainable design elements into the project, so that the homes would be energy-efficient and have low maintenance costs for their residents. The Collaborative provided a service grant to help Habitat develop its first affordable green housing project, and WRT continued its relationship with Habitat as a consultant, providing the final design and construction documentation and management.

Building the future: During a volunteer work day, architect Maarten Pesch explains the green features of the Stiles Street housing to a future owner/resident.

Design

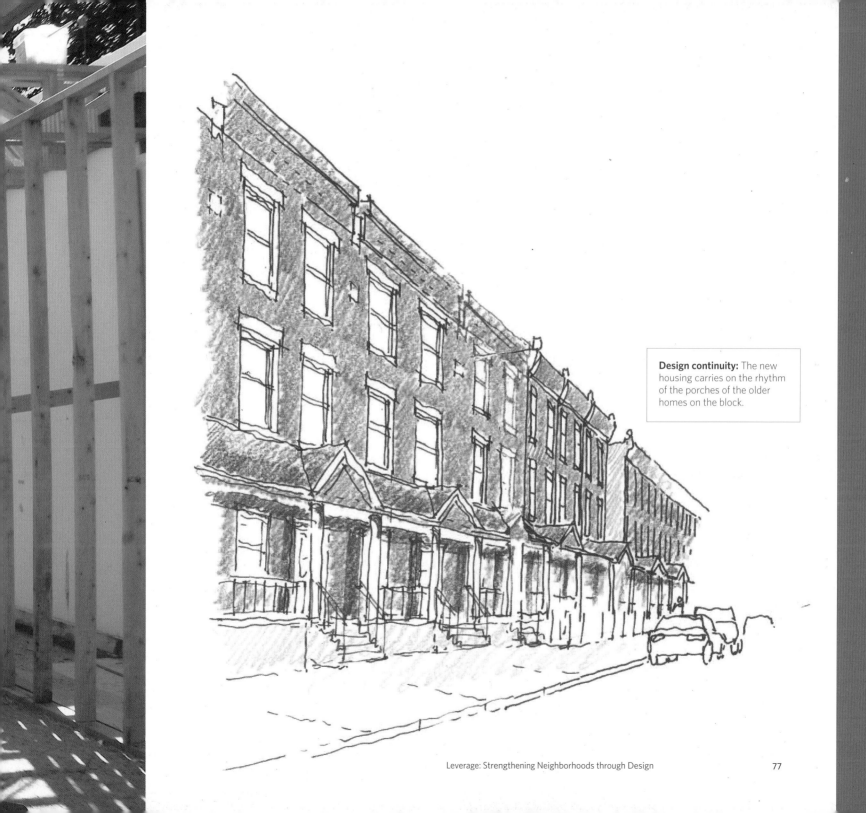

Design continuity: The new housing carries on the rhythm of the porches of the older homes on the block.

Creating a Neighborhood Anchor:
Simons Recreation Center

Design

Location
7200 Woolston Ave. (at Walnut Ln.), West Oak Lane neighborhood, Philadelphia

Services completed
1993

Client
Simons Recreation Center Advisory Council

Volunteers
Dori Bova, AIA, Jan Lucas Strouse, AIA, Robert Bole

Products
Programming study, conceptual preliminary cost estimate

Consultant for final design
Studio Agoos Lovera

Built
2000

This is a story of a recreation center at the heart of a neighborhood that was in turnaround mode: West Oak Lane. "Simons Rec" was bursting at the seams with use by residents, for programs that were helping to rebuild the community. But, with an ice rink dating from 1948 and a main building from the 1970s, they needed a design plan that was also forward thinking.

Design Facilitates Unity

By the early 1990s, a decade of effort to revitalize this working-class, predominantly African-American community was bearing fruit. As a result, the Simons Rec advisory board needed a project proposal showing how they sought to grow to make a strong case for funding. And they did, raising $2.1 million in state funding, with the help of State Rep. Dwight Evans. They hired the firm of Studio Agoos Lovera for the final design, which was completed in 2000.

The Collaborative's proposal focused on massing more than design: how much space was needed for specific activities and where to expand. The predesign process helped the advisory board to collaborate with residents to create a vision for an infrastructure that aligned with the future needs of the community. The people of West Oak Lane came together as well—in active resistance to the breakdown of community that all-to-often depletes city neighborhoods like this one.

Making it work: Amid a climate of budget cutbacks, an essential aspect of the project's success was the involvement of the City's Department of Parks and Recreation. Then-commissioner Mike DiBerardinis was particularly focused on improving neighborhood rec centers like this one, and helped to issue the request for proposals (RFP) for Simons. Findings from the Collaborative's study were included in the RFP to convey the project scope and the advisory council's input.

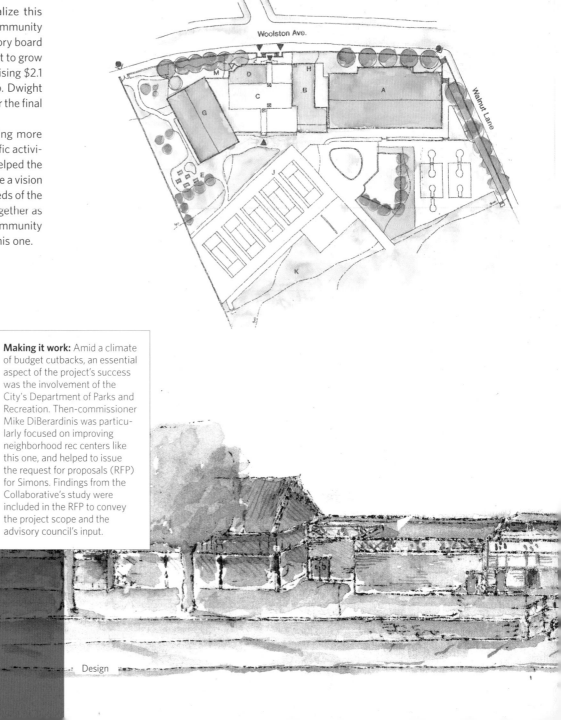

Design

"West Oak Lane is a key neighborhood to preserve and develop. There are good, strong, workingclass people moving into the neighborhood and living there. These are people we want to keep in the city. We compete with the suburbs for them. Neighborhoods like Ogontz are a barometer of how the city is doing."
—*Jeremy Nowak, Delaware Valley Community Reinvestment Fund* (quoted in the Philadelphia Inquirer, *September 15, 1996)*

A 360° View, Part III:
Where the Collaborative Should Go from Here

The Project-Formation Business

Todd Woodward: **How can the Collaborative ensure that the work we do means something? With some of the projects, we wonder whether they will go anywhere. Education matters to us, but as volunteers, we also want to make a difference. Are there ways the organization can do more of this?**

Alan Greenberger: The Collaborative can…perfect what it does pretty well already: be selective about the projects you take on. It can afford to up its scale. The Collaborative should always do architectural projects on behalf of people who have buildings and an idea, but [there's opportunity to pursue] some of the [different areas] you have started to veer into, [such as] filling in gaps one block at a time, handling larger sites. The Collaborative has a role to play in **being smart about which projects you do**, with the specific intent of forming the collective will that enables good things to happen.

In the early days of organizations like the Collaborative, there was always an anxiety that the Collaborative is providing for free services that [design] professionals should provide. One way to counter that argument is to show that **what you are doing is trying to build the will to get something done**—and envisioning that at a fairly basic level is part of building organizational strength.

You're in the project formation business. The work of the Collaborative is in building the collective will and organizational strength around a project that wants to be done. This distinguishes its role from taking work from professionals, which is certainly not the business the Collaborative is in. I spend all my time worrying about getting to the stage where there *is* a project. This is really hard, and [one of my duties is to] rearrange [City] staff [to target] planned areas of the city, [in an attempt] to extract projects from them. But as a city—and I'm sure this is true of most resources—we don't have the resources to meet the demand that is likely to be out there. It's just not possible.

Maurice Cox: **There are very few places where those who are interested in advancing an idea for a project can go**—other than the regulatory public process—to come to some kind of a shared vision with community stakeholders. It's an enormous burden on the City—on City staff or a department—to go out and create public will, or be the broker between the development interest and the community interest.

Groups like the Collaborative are the obvious neutral ground that can do that kind of preparatory work. It's an essential component: getting projects from an idea to some broad consensus.

Making Cities the Client

Todd: **Alan said earlier that the Collaborative might broaden the scale of what it takes on, and we've also talked about taking on smaller projects. If you both had a crystal ball, what advice would you offer? What will be the key issues the Collaborative might tackle?**

Alan: There's an opportunity for the Collaborative to **think of the City as a client** from time to time. You've always relied on projects coming from grass roots, and that will always be the core of what you do. But think of it the other way around. What if I said you could organize a highly motivated group of volunteers to look at a problem that we have and that we in City government don't have the staff to do it? I could unload a list of ten things right now that young volunteer design folks would have a great time with, exploring an idea, unleashing a latent potential that we don't have time to think about, other than this intuition that there's something there.

Todd: That's an excellent idea. Can I sign up to be on that team?

Beth Miller: Design Trust in New York has been very successful with these types of partnerships.

Maurice: In Virginia we legislate every five years to update our comprehensive plan and plan process. We decided to turn over to the community design center that process of leading these neighborhood discussions on everything that is in a comprehensive plan, and then in turn to train young design advocates in facilitating discussions around a wide variety of neighborhood topics. It was the most energetic, empowering comprehensive planning process we ever had, because we were able to hold dozens of conversations at the scale of [individual] neighborhoods.

Then we were able to stand back and look at what people said, and they fell into a series of reoccurring values that—lo and behold—crossed all neighborhoods. Rather than a top-down "What are our values?" meeting, we risked asking people in groups of 25 or 50, and then [looked] to see whether there was any commonality. Of course there was. **We got to a vision for our city that came out of many conversations instead of one.**

I remember doubts we had along the lines of, "What happens when one neighborhood stands for this [issue], and another neighborhood stands for that [issue]?" It showed that there are certain core values that people identify with as a community, and it may be different in Philadelphia than it is in Charlottesville. Having a process that is not [run by] the City—but in which the City is understood as more of a global convener—turned out to be very powerful. It was literally a contract that the City made with the design center for comprehensive planning.

Todd: I love the idea of the City as a client. It touches on the idea of the Collaborative would be providing, in essence, time for reflection that you don't have in doing the day-to-day business that you have to do.

Alan: Virginia has a five-year mandate for comprehensive planning? Philadelphia has a 50-year mandate. We're doing the first comprehensive plan in 50 years.

Beth: There are going to be 18 neighborhood district plans, and great opportunities to work with individuals in the neighborhoods where they are, and respond to their hopes and aspirations.

Maurice: Pittsburgh is doing its first comprehensive plan in 50 years. What do you make of that? Has comprehensive planning been dead in Pennsylvania?

Beth: We're giving it a resuscitation.

Alan: There must be a 50-year [trend] in Pennsylvania—something in the water, because there are consistent patterns that happen on each side of the state.

Beth: Generational turnover.

Alan: Without getting into the whole politics/sociology of it, I think it reflects pretty accurately the cycle of beliefs in planning from the 1950s and 1960s to the abrogation of planning, through the removal of federal money, and an unwillingness (at least on the part of the great Rust Belt cities) to step up into the void and fund planning. So for Philadelphia, it actually became anti-planning, top-down planning, community empowerment—the death and life of great American cities but also populist politicians. It was Philadelphia Mayor Frank Rizzo saying, "You don't have to listen to those knuckleheads (who work for me)! Do what you want to do." Then it went through the era of hero developers, and then it morphed (at least in this city) into strong deal-making politicians who didn't do planning either because they did deals in their offices—private sector heroism. It's a kind of Reagan follow-on.

Seizing Philadelphia's "Planning Moment"

Todd: **What opportunities do you see for the Collaborative given the current political climate in the city?**

Maurice: You [in Philadelphia] have come to an incredible place where you now are going [through] the Urban Land Institute (ULI) roof. Mayor Nutter believes in planning and is hosting the Mayors' Institute on City Design, and he's putting an architect [Alan Greenberger] at the head of his planning operation. Up until a couple of years ago, Andy Altman was there. It's an incredible difference in your current mayor's belief in the power of planning.

Alan: Mayor Nutter also gets criticized for being too process-oriented. [The establishment] kind of liked the "deal" days [of some previous administrations], because it looked like things got done quickly. In fact, in prior decades, over-ambition probably jammed up more critical property than people realize. But it's very American to esteem an individual who's seen as making the deals.

One of the better City Council members was overheard criticizing me—not to me, of course—saying, "Well, Alan's a nice guy, but he's an architect, he's not a deal guy." Meanwhile, I'm thinking, "Yeah, but deals are getting done. How do you think they're happening?" It's not necessarily by me being a big hero, but I have a team of people who are all part of a network of how these things happen; it's not the classic quarterback method, but they are getting done.

Maurice: How do you think Mayor Nutter's year as a Rose Fellow has changed how he understands the power of what your office is able to do?

Alan: I have nothing but good things to say about his year with the Rose Fellows. Not only did they actually help, but they allowed us to take an area that we intuitively thought needed attention [North Broad Street] and put it squarely on the mayor's agenda. He hadn't been hostile to this work, but as a mayor he's thinking about all sorts of things. And we were able to say, "This is now a critical area." I knew we had it when, toward the end of the Rose year, an LA investor—a sort of venture capitalist of planning—shows up in our midst and says, "Mayor, I'm thinking I'd like to invest in Philadelphia. What are you thinking about?" And without even flinching, Mayor Nutter

says, "North Broad Street," which was our Rose topic. He asks the investor, "What are you doing for the next two hours? Let's drive up and down the street."

Maurice: And he could probably talk about it with incredible insight and in a very persuasive way, and that's really what it's all about—the capacity of our political leaders to do it. One of the things that I hope that the Collaborative does is build on the fact that you have a design advocate in City Hall who understands the value of what you do—and potentially would entertain a proposal from you that, two years ago, maybe he would not.

Beth: I think Maurice is making the ask for me, Alan!

Maurice: You know that these [opportunities] are moments in time—that there are things that align—and it's really hard to remember that [those opportunities] are not going to be there forever. You feel an obligation to exploit it to get something done. I'm speaking nostalgically of what we did here in Charlottesville, [when I] realized there was a moment in time—and a series of people—when things aligned, and we were able to advance some very big ideas. And then that moment disappeared, and that was the end of it. Fortunately we had taken advantage of that moment.

In Philadelphia you are all in a similar moment, and you had better exploit it to the fullest, because you cannot assume that [in the next administration] you will have another mayor who will be just as interested in design issues, or that Alan will remain in his position for the next 20 years. You can't count on any of that, so if you [bring to it] the sense of urgency there is now that allows us to start

things, it will support thinking big and thinking in our transformative way. That would really be my wish for the Design Center: [given that] these moments are incredibly fleeting, you have to take advantage of them as they present themselves.

Alan: I couldn't agree more. I have become keenly aware of the fleetingness of the moment. Right now, we'll get four more years out of this (so effectively we'll get four and a half more years out of this), and then the moment could truly be over, **to the extent that we can institutionalize certain good practices, that's a big gift to the future.** And to the extent we can't, we have better [accomplish] something in those years.

Institutionalizing Good Design

Todd: **How else do you see the Collaborative's role evolving?**

Maurice: One of the things that you all are able to do [in Philadelphia]—because of your a size and [the fact that] you have enough public commissions that you can do good—is begin to understand the notion of how you proffer good design.

The City of New York has figured out a way to create a design excellence program that is pretty robust and is starting to give the city a status of promoting extraordinary design excellence in public commissions.

It's one thing to do it in the public sector;

you can create requests for qualifications and you can legally create a pool of people prequalified to do the commission, so the public can set the bar. But the real challenge is how to get the private sector to push design as a value to [factor into] their equation in those projects. Just like we have affordable housing proffers, and all kinds of open space proffers, one wonders whether you could have a "good design" proffer, where people who are developing contribute to a pot that could be used in innovative ways to raise the bar in design excellence in the private sector.

Beth: You'd have to define "design excellence."

Alan: I think how to institutionalize that is what I'm really not clear about. On a day-to-day basis [in Philadelphia], it happens to a large degree because there's a small cadre of us who just keep talking about it. It's interesting—it does embed itself in places where you would not otherwise expect it. My colleagues and some of the other deputy mayors keep hammering at it.

The other nice thing that's happening—at least in the private sector—is that the demand side is going up. So, where it shows up most noticeably is in buildings designed to high sustainability standards, where one developer in town says, "I'm never building another building that's not LEED Gold or Platinum because that's my client base, and I can't build otherwise." It's even showing up now in industrial buildings that they do, because other developers see that and think about it.

Beth: Raising the bar.

Maurice: I think that the public has role to play, because if the City says, "We're not building another community center, another pool, another school that's not LEED Gold or Platinum," that automatically gets telegraphed to the private sector. So if you're saying, "We're practicing what we preach, we're asking you to do what we do," that goes an enormous way. Our public buildings can't look like crap if we want the private sector to produce extraordinary works of architecture. Our stuff has to actually be the best stuff.

Creating a culture where design is of real value is really what the Collaborative does, and continues to do, in terms of organizing design advocates to make sure that the case is always being put in front of the general public, so they hear people talking about design. I can't tell you what a difference that makes, particularly in a city like Philadelphia, where you have such a strong design community creating a way, so there is always a conversation about design. **You raise the overall community discussion about the built environment.**

A lot of times it's through critical public projects that the mayor may have on his agenda—I think those are always the best—or things that are coming up in the private sector. Alan knows the community will need to have a really robust conversation about design, so he reaches out to the Collaborative and says, "Can you set the stage for this conversation?" Whether it's this particular area or a particular building, it's part of creating a culture.

As much as I try to institutionalize good design, in the end I've found that the best institution you can create is **a constant stream of high-quality designers who are in positions of confidence with people who make decisions.** I'm not sure what planning boards or design review boards help the planning office, but make sure that you have the highest-quality design professionals volunteering to serve on those boards and commissions. Or ensuring that there is an easy pipeline between the schools of architecture and their leadership, and the kind of council that works with the planning office and City Hall, to break down the silos that tend to exist between those different organizations. In Philadelphia the leadership of some of the universities have had really good participation. But again—**it's about getting designers who have really strong and thoughtful reflections on the city in the company of political leaders and decision makers, so that this conversation about design can flow from that.**

Alan: Beth is our most recent planning commissioner. She's one of nine. Six are appointments by the mayor, and three are appointments from finance, the managing director, and the commerce department, who all have reserved seats.

Maurice: Alan, at some point I'd love to see what you're excited about coming down the pike. I know that lots of projects have been put on hold, but they're going to come back and I'd be really interested to know what's been keeping you excited over this next four and half years.

Alan: I'd love to have that conversation.

Beth: There will be an opportunity for that at the national conference of the Association of Architecture Organizations, the Architecture and Design Education Network, and the Association for Community Design—a joint conference of all three organizations we're hosting October 9–11, 2011. Hopefully you can have more of this discussion in front of some of your colleagues, and tell the Philadelphia story from that national perspective.

BY SALLY HARRISON

At the Margins:
Politics and Design Now

THE CALL TO CITIZEN PARTICIPATION IN DESIGN, once revolutionary, has developed in myriad interesting ways since it was first articulated in the 1960s. This foundation of the community design movement has expanded the agency of the design professions. Designers have realized thousands of projects like those the Community Design Collaborative undertakes, thereby engaging the members of a community in an empowering discursive method of design.[1] These new community design activisms are emerging in *reactive*, *proactive*, and *trans*active ways, each of which has a role to play in the evolving political, cultural, and physical landscapes.

This Moment in Design Activism

A new wave of political and spatial issues is cresting, and new practices in social design are taking shape in response. Globalization of capital is accelerating disinvestment in local economies, undermining communal structures, and making housing less and less available to needy populations. Environmental degradation generates epidemic health problems and threatens food security, especially at the margins of our society, making evident the spatial injustices embedded in the physical environment. As designers who work at the margins, community designers are prepared to act with authority and purpose—to be activists and to recognize that our work is an essential act in building democracy. Only now, in the face of global economic crisis, is the cult of the star architect and elite client receding, having dominated the mediated world over the last three decades. Only now are we expanding the concept of "public" to include the vast majority of the population that has little or no access to the service of

designers or to designed environments themselves. It is an opportune moment to recognize our growing strengths and also revisit the role of political activism as a unifying agenda of contemporary social design.[2]

Activism in design can begin with students bearing witness to inequity and institutionalized injustice through community-based studio and research projects. Or it can take the form of leadership within the political apparatus of cities by architects and planners like Jaime Lerner in Curitiba, David Gouverneur in Caracas, and now Alan Greenberger in Philadelphia, who have used their agency to place strategies for urban social sustainability at the forefront of public discourse and action. In between (and sometimes linked with) the institutions of learning and leadership, a cornucopia of design activisms are emerging that operate in *reactive*, *proactive*, and *trans*active ways. Typical of reactive practices are the professional service grants like those that form the core of the Collaborative's work, but also disaster relief efforts and design-build projects. The proactive model of practice frames critical issues through the use of charrettes, temporary art-based spatial practices, and speculative design research. Transactive community design engages in long-term commitment to a specific locale, building relationships of people to place around the design process.

The Evolution of Contemporary Community Design:
The Collaborative in Context

In 1963 the Architects Renewal Committee of Harlem (ARCH) gathered to protest a highway planned to run through northern Manhattan that would bisect a poor black neighborhood. The group's cohesion around advocacy for the rights of the local community in face of the juggernaut of top-down city planning evolved to form one of the earliest prototypes for the community design center, opening new roles for designers and planners.[3]

Advocates formed centers in Baltimore, New York, Cincinnati, and other cities in the U.S. as well as in Europe and the U.K., providing design and planning services to newly emerging community development corporations. Recalibrating power relations, these nongovernmental intermediaries formed the client base for much of the early community design work. The Philadelphia chapter of the American Institute of Architects (AIA) established one of the first of these centers, the Architect's Workshop, in 1968. In operation for more than 15 years, the Workshop offered the pro bono services of AIA members to neighborhood organizations in Philadelphia, and as such was very much the forerunner of the Collaborative.

In the late 1960s advocacy for disenfranchised communities took political center stage in public design discourse. It was a tumultuous time steeped in adversarial rhetoric. With clearly demarked lines of resistance and incantations of "power to the people," the early advocacy planners were militantly reactive, using their agency to combat the well-funded threat of politically single-minded municipal projects. But having burst on the scene with much éclat, the community design movement kept a relatively low profile in the succeeding decades, especially during the politically conservative 1980s, when funding to cities was drastically reduced. Community advocacy had lost its bully pulpit, and a socially progressive agenda was relegated to the margins of our design culture. A period of speculation in both theory and practice upended an ethos of sociopolitical action through design, and widespread apathy toward those living in poverty took hold. In his 1984 book *The Scope of Social Architecture,* Richard Hatch cites Alex Tzonis and Liane Lefaivre's blistering critique of the then-current professional/academic narcissism: "The preoccupation with formalism, hedonism, graphism, and elitism has allowed architects to shift with easy conscience from practical measures to the realm of mental constructs."[4]

The founding of the Collaborative in 1991 anticipated a resurgence of social activism in the design professions. Many of the issues that were prominent twenty-five years earlier were still present, or worse: widespread urban poverty, violent crime, race-based geographic disparity, and lack of access to affordable housing. Sensing the vacuum created by the closing of the Architect's Workshop, the Philadelphia chapter of the AIA had hosted a Regional/Urban Design Action Team (R/UDAT) visit to focus on the deteriorated post-industrial neighborhoods in central North Philadelphia. The local AIA committee worked for months on the ground with the communities, the City, and local political leaders to set the stage for a highly public urban forum to put forth North Philadelphia's critical issues and a framework for envisioning its future.

The R/UDAT was an intensely proactive process. Over the course a four-day charrette, the nationally fielded team of designers, economists, and political activists worked with the local AIA and its community-based participants. The process discredited widely held myths about North Philadelphia, proposed new urban strategies, and unearthed scores of nascent and potential development projects. In the wake of the R/UDAT team's departure, we in Philadelphia considered how to build on this momentum, and before long we were running housing and urban design studios at Temple University and at the University of Pennsylvania. And within the AIA, the idea of the Community Design Collaborative was born.

Leveraging Reactive Practice

Pro bono community design centers like the Collaborative—which was formed in response to the very tangible needs for design services that emerged from the R/UDAT—commonly adhere to what I'm calling a reactive model. This suggests that they follow the traditional role of the design professions in responding to a situation or program that others have defined extrinsically. The work, though certainly not apolitical, does not directly engage the designers in a political process. Projects usually have a limited scope in terms of the inquiry and the potential for deep engagement with the end users of the projects. Yet in several decades of work, community design centers have established a visible and viable alternative practice, intended expressly for those whom design professions have historically underserved. This practice has brought numerous architects, planners, engineers, and landscape architects into a larger cultural ethos of design for the public good.

Reactive practice may also coalesce in response to an external threat, as during the formative years of the community design movement. On the world stage—responding to the ravages of human and nonhuman forces—disaster relief is perhaps the purest form of current reactive design work. Motivated by humanitarian impulses, the designers bring idealism and creative problem-solving skills to bear on the decomposition of spatial networks and, indirectly, extraordinary human suffering. Shigeru Ban's elegantly modest constructions for housing in the aftermath of the Kobe earthquake inspired a generation of designers with this kind of humanitarian intervention.[5]

Developing Proactive Practice

To address crises that we can reasonably anticipate designers can employ a proactive approach to raise questions, initiate action, and engage the political establishments. Design professionals can also use proactive means to understand patterns of social injustice and, now, the impact of climate change, on inhabited environments of all kinds. Open-ended charrettes like the R/UDAT and by-invitation speculative projects such as the Collaborative's Infill Philadelphia address current and emerging issues in practice. Proactive practice often exists outside the professional setting, in the realm of academia, using research, critical writing, speculation, and experimental techniques to represent the complex ecologies of place. Social philosopher-critics like Mike Davis and David Harvey have advanced critical discourse on the ecologies of inequality.[6] Their writings expose the political impact of the neoliberal economic structure on marginalized urban communities, where the private realm has consumed public space.

Visual representation of place is an emerging and powerful form of proactive discourse that is disseminated in books and public exhibitions. These representations address the dynamic systems—social, environmental, economic, and political—that underlie the social occupation of space. Anuradha Mathur and Dilip da Cunha, principals of a design firm based in Philadelphia and Bangalore, concentrate on issue-centered public investigations around questions of inhabitation in territories dominated by their natural hydrologies. In their words: "Activist practice means first that we are initiators. Rather than waiting for a commissioned project, we ask the first question, frame the issue, and propose possibilities. Our purpose is to affect change, from policy to pedagogy right down to how people image and imagine environments, both built and natural."[7]

The work of Laura Kurgan and Columbia University's Spatial Information Design Lab is similarly proactive and directed at public policy. The lab has mapped criminal justice data in several major cities, demonstrating a chilling concentration of incarcerated people from specific urban neighborhoods: "The Million Dollar Blocks." Referring to the costs of housing inmates, the project compares the spending on education, healthcare, housing, and pro-social programs that, if equally well funded, might preclude the devastating effects of an institutionally supported criminal culture on these neighborhoods. Their compelling GIS-generated images have been exhibited at the Museum of Modern Art in New York and the National Constitution Center in Philadelphia.

The Next Frontier: Transactive Practice

To address the issues that underlie building more democratic environments and truly engage all our publics, a vigorously transactive design model may be most effective. This takes time. Within this model, the act of designing and the products of design form an unfolding discourse. As designers, we neither abandon our role as knowledgeable professionals nor permit ourselves safe distance from the struggle, but rather must, in Timothy Morton's words, "hang out in what feels like dualism…and admit we have a choice."[8]

Sustained engagement in the ecology of a particular community underlies the transactive practice model. The renowned activist Teddy Cruz says we must "focus on the issues of the local…Every issue converges there." Negotiation around the very tangible conditions of space and place are the drivers of design democracy, and they have the existential power to "trickle up" and transform often hardened policies that obstruct development of livable space.[9]

The Urban Workshop at Temple University, like a number of other university-based centers, has committed to multiyear partnerships with neighborhoods at the university's margins. We have worked with our community partners and unmasked the processes of design, research, and production—weaving together neighborhood plans and policy frameworks, designing and building homes, and installing gardens and art. Engaging the multiple systems that form a community, we work at many scales and draw on the resources of diverse disciplines and agents. We are simultaneously teachers and learners, creative experts and interpreters, researchers and laborers.

"Activist practice means first that we are initiators. Rather than waiting for a commissioned project, we ask the first question, frame the issue, and propose possibilities."
—Anuradha Mathur and Dilip da Cunha

At the Margins

Transactive social design uncovers embedded cultural value, allowing an often-modest reality to inform and guide development. In his planning and design work in poor communities in the global South, educator and practitioner Nabeel Hamdi has sought change through catalyzing the "emergent potential" found in the often self-made, everyday lived world. Treading a careful balance between facilitating design actions and allowing self-organizing systems to take hold, Hamdi and his colleagues prepare the ground for change and open doors to partners outside the community. In one project they find a bus stop, where a critical density of interaction takes place, and set in motion small, deft interventions: trees for shade, street lighting, and an improved standpipe, to help develop a vibrant center of community. Hamdi declares that, in the interest of change, practice disturbs the order of things, yet "*intelligent practice* builds on the collective wisdom of people and organizations on the ground—those who think locally and act locally—which is then rationalized in ways that make a difference globally... One starts with something small and one starts where it counts."[10]

Design Activism at the Center and the Margins

The community design movement appears to have arrived once again at center stage. Organizations like the Collaborative have become established, respected institutions that engage the broad participation of private practitioners and nonprofit clients alike. In some city governments, creative and enlightened policymakers are building an ethos of democracy around the planning and design of urban space. And in the vanguard of design culture, the publication of a spate of new books[11] and high-profile exhibitions are exploring and documenting the resurgence of a collective social awareness.

But even as we count these successes, it is important also to push outward from the center and continue to engage the margins, where the weave of social fabric has unraveled and which present the most pressing challenges to a democratic way of life. Going back and forth between the center and the margins, we the Collaborative (as well as architects in general) can maintain a critical perspective and use design where it counts most, knowing when and how reactive, proactive, or transactive practice will be most appropriate and/or effective. Such a multifaceted approach invites more participants with varied talents to enlist in the project of social change. A diverse array of practitioners can engage the whole ecology of design through agility and imagination, technical expertise, design inventiveness, interpersonal skills, and the ability to represent complex issues visually. And our communities, in all their complexity, are poised to join as full partners in this creative process. Community design, then, is neither the conscience of our professions, nor the next wave of fashion, but a powerful agent of revitalization—one that opens new horizons for architecture, planning, and design.

1 Giancarlo De Carlo, "Architecture's Public" in *Architecture and Participation,* ed. Peter Blundell Jones, Doina Petrescu, and Jeremy Till (London: Routledge, 2005), 3–22.

2 Jose L. S. Gamez and Susan Rogers, "An Architecture of Change" in *Expanding Architecture: Design as Activism,* ed. Bryan Bell and Katie Wakeford (New York: Metropolis Books, 2008), 22. See also: Andres Lepik, *Small Scale, Big Change: New Architectures of Social Engagement* (New York: Museum of Modern Art, 2010).

3 See: http://spatialagency.net/database

4 C. Richard Hatch, ed., *The Scope of Social Architecture* (New York: Van Nostrand Rheinhold, 1984), 3.

5 Occasionally problematic in the reactive practice of disaster reconstruction is the dual temptation to impose a new utopian vision (uncannily exhuming Le Corbusier's insistence on the "cleared site") and to seize a high-profile opportunity for design celebrity. These have been both evident in post-Katrina New Orleans and in the postwar interventions in Serbia Herzegovina. See "Facts on the Ground: Urbanism from Midroad to Ditch" by Michelle Provoost and Wouter Vanstiphout in *Urban Design,* ed. Alex Krieger and William Saunders (Minneapolis: University of Minnesota Press, 2009), 186–97, and Architecture for Humanity's *Design Like You Give a Damn: Architectural Responses to Humanitarian Crises,* ed. Kate Stohr and Cameron Sinclair (New York: Metropolis Books, 2006).

6 Richard LeGates and Frederic Stout, eds., introduction to "Contested Cities: Social Process and Spatial Form" by David Harvey, in *The City Reader,* 4th ed. (New York: Routledge, 2007), 226.

7 See: http://places.designobserver.com/feature/preparing-ground-an-interview-with-anuradha-mathur-and-dilip-da-cunha/13858/

8 Timothy Morton, *Ecology without Nature: Rethinking Environmental Aesthetics* (Cambridge, Mass.: Harvard University Press, 2007), 205.

9 See: http://tmagazine.blogs.nytimes.com/2010/01/21/the-nifty-50-teddy-cruz-architect

10 Nabeel Hamdi, *Small Change: About the Art of Practice and the Limits of Planning in Cities* (London: Earthscan, 2004), xviii.

11 John Cary, ed., *The Power of Pro Bono: 40 Stories about Design for the Public Good by Architects and Their Clients* (New York: Metropolis Books, 2010).

COLLABORATION

All of the Collaborative's projects embody the spirit and ethic of collaboration, yet some of our projects have opened new doors for individuals and organizations to learn from each other. This section highlights unique partnerships among groups that might not otherwise have worked together toward a shared vision.

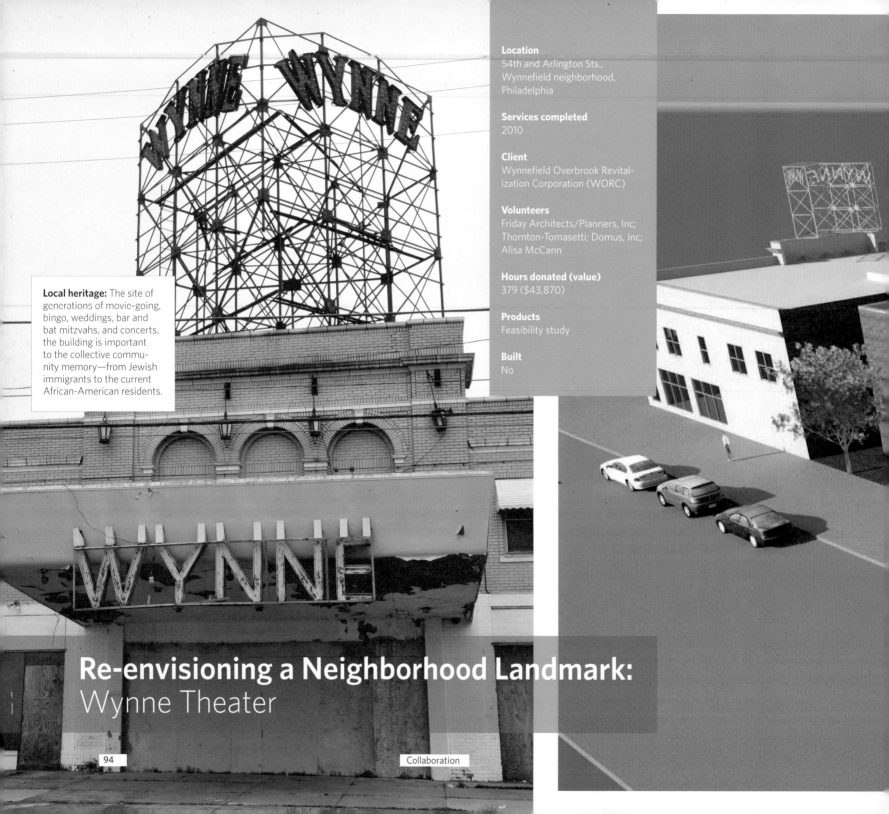

Location
54th and Arlington Sts.,
Wynnefield neighborhood,
Philadelphia

Services completed
2010

Client
Wynnefield Overbrook Revitalization Corporation (WORC)

Volunteers
Friday Architects/Planners, Inc;
Thornton-Tomasetti; Domus, Inc;
Alisa McCann

Hours donated (value)
379 ($43,870)

Products
Feasibility study

Built
No

Local heritage: The site of generations of movie-going, bingo, weddings, bar and bat mitzvahs, and concerts, the building is important to the collective community memory—from Jewish immigrants to the current African-American residents.

Re-envisioning a Neighborhood Landmark:
Wynne Theater

Collaboration

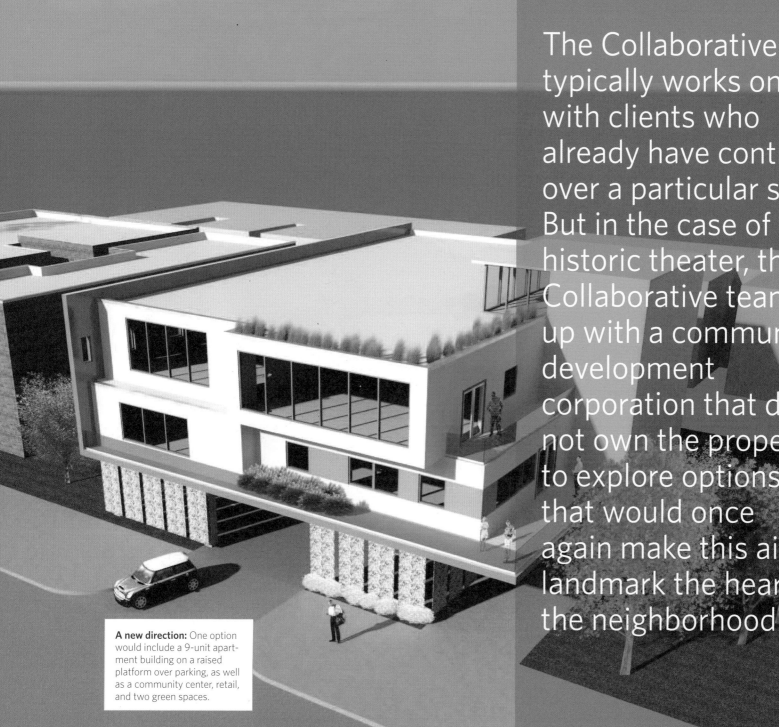

The Collaborative typically works only with clients who already have control over a particular site. But in the case of this historic theater, the Collaborative teamed up with a community development corporation that did not own the property, to explore options that would once again make this ailing landmark the heart of the neighborhood.

A new direction: One option would include a 9-unit apartment building on a raised platform over parking, as well as a community center, retail, and two green spaces.

Reclaiming a Source of Community Pride

WORC described the empty, neglected building—which had been developed as a movie theater in 1928 and was used as a ballroom and a banquet hall in later inceptions—as the "only impediment in an otherwise stable neighborhood, once a source of community pride." The Collaborative study sought to explore potential reuses given the disrepair and the fact that many original architectural details had been destroyed.

The team found that the theater headhouse—a foyer with a Renaissance Revival facade flanked by retail space—could be rescued with relatively modest improvements. They also determined that the main theater space, covering about two-thirds of the site, should be demolished to make way for new development that brought new purpose to the main entrance.

Two Feasible Design Options

The Collaborative led three interactive workshops to identify four redevelopment scenarios, exploring two in more depth: a community center with meeting, classroom, and gathering space, and a mixed-use project featuring nine new apartment units.

Both scenarios would retain and refurbish the theater headhouse— with its handsome foyer, old-school storefronts, and distinctive sign. The rental housing option was deemed to be more feasible, given that the building will need to be almost entirely revenue producing.

Determining Suitability for Government Resources

The Collaborative prides itself on helping clients navigate the world of funders and resources. This feasibility study sought to explore whether the site was applicable to a recently passed state conservation act, which could appoint a conservator to assume responsibility for stabilizing and adapting the site for productive use. It became clear through the predesign process that, although the building satisfied the physical requirements, its complicated structure, ownership, and the extent of deterioration meant that pursuing this source of support was not the best use of WORC's time.

Collaboration

Keeping the icon: Another proposed strategy was to perform partial demolition in order to keep the theater headhouse, but create space for a more ambitious community center.

Nourishing a Neighborhood:
Weavers Way Ogontz

First of its kind: West Oak Lane was a pilot location for a new network of satellite co-ops in underserved neighborhoods, in this case inspired by the opportunity to lease a two-story building.

FRUIT OF THE SPIRIT
PRODUCE STORE
EAT FRESH EAT SMART!!

Church of Broken Pieces

Collaboration

This project sought to reinvent a typical storefront as a community resource for fresh, locally grown food and a healthy lifestyle. The West Oak Lane neighborhood—much admired for striving to maintain the quality of its housing, schools, and playground—offered little in the way of fresh produce. The nearest outlet was an eleven-minute walk away from Ogontz Avenue, the neighborhood's main shopping street, out of the back of a truck. The design team re-envisioned the building and an adjacent lot as a living organism—one that can grow and evolve as the community becomes increasingly engaged in the food co-op.

Location
2129 North 72nd Ave. (at Ogontz Ave.), West Oak Lane neighborhood, Philadelphia

Services completed
2008

Client
Weavers Way Community Programs; Ogontz Avenue Revitalization Corporation

Volunteers
Studio Agoos Lovera

Hours donated (value)
535 ($40,205)

Products
Conceptual design for three phases of expansion

Sustainable design features
Phase 2: green screen; phase 3: stair tower providing passive cooling, green roof, sun shading

Built
No

Infill Philadelphia Partners
The Reinvestment Fund; The Food Trust

Leverage: Strengthening Neighborhoods through Design

"Infilling" with Strong Design

Weavers Way Ogontz was one of several projects of the Collaborative's Infill Philadelphia, a multi-phased design initiative that helps urban communities reinvent their neighborhoods and rethink the use of older spaces. This aspect of a phase of Infill focused on food access for urban neighborhoods.

Creating Flexible, Functional Security

The conceptual plan outlined a strategy for the co-op to expand in phases—adding more retail space, a demonstration kitchen, a green roof, and even a café over time; the third phase considers full expansion onto the adjacent vacant lot, to optimize the co-op's potential.

The early design featured an innovative security grille that could enliven any urban commercial corridor. Inspired by the metal security grilles that shutter many city storefronts after hours, the design team fabricated perforated metal panels that fold out during the day to create an open-air produce stand and overhead canopy. At night the panels fold back to secure the facade, while also allowing light from inside the store to illuminate the sidewalk, creating a more open and safer atmosphere for pedestrians.

PERSPECTIVE

Expanding the reach of fresh food: The new store is a satellite of Weavers Way, a Philadelphia food co-op that sought to establish a branch within reach of moderate-income families.

"We want to help residents in the community feel like they own a piece of the co-op."
—*Alex Chan,*
Agoos Lovera Studio

Design team (left to right): Ted Agoos, Eriberto Luis Cruz (of Weavers Way), Eddie Layton, Wandy Chang, Adam Jeckel, Brian Tiede, and Alex Chan

Leverage: Strengthening Neighborhoods through Design

101

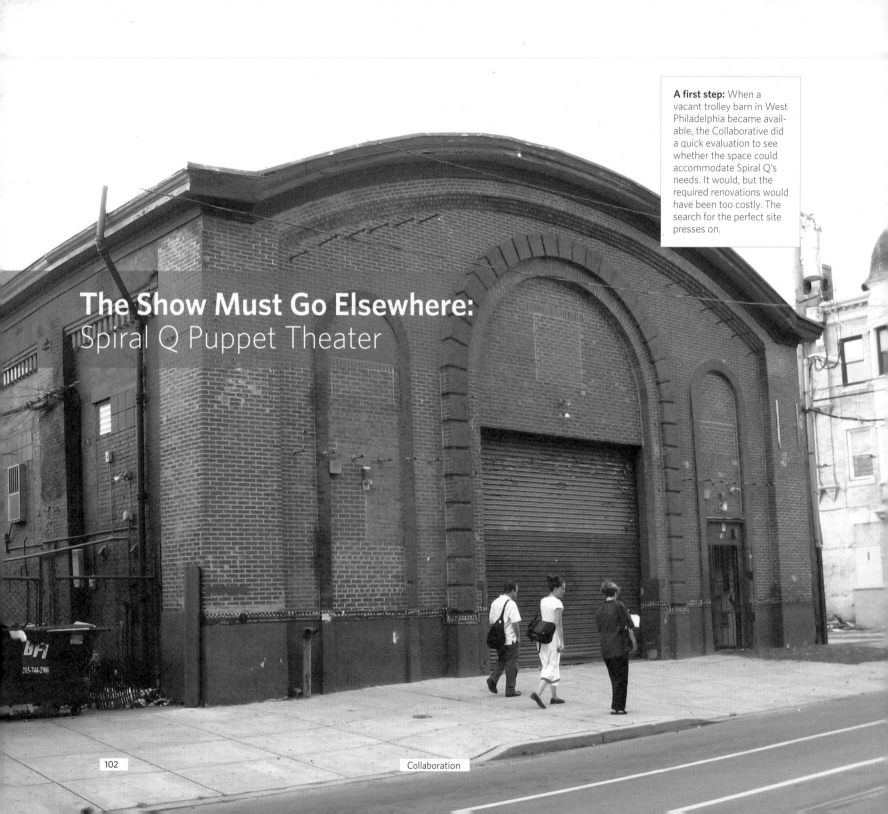

The Show Must Go Elsewhere:
Spiral Q Puppet Theater

A first step: When a vacant trolley barn in West Philadelphia became available, the Collaborative did a quick evaluation to see whether the space could accommodate Spiral Q's needs. It would, but the required renovations would have been too costly. The search for the perfect site presses on.

A performing arts group forced to relocate from its industrial space—with a tremendous amount of bulky and delicate equipment in tow— equaled a fun challenge for the Collaborative. Many nonprofits face this daunting task alone, but the Collaborative has assisted Spiral Q Puppet Theater since 2005 to evaluate potential sites for their suitability. It's an inspiring process as Spiral Q plans for continued growth.

Location
Various

Services completed
Ongoing as of 2011

Client
Spiral Q Puppet Theater

Volunteers
KieranTimberlake Associates, LLP; Duffield Associates, Inc.; Marvin Waxman Consulting Engineers; Becker & Frondorf; Brian Szymanik Architects; International Consultants, Inc.

Hours donated (value)
133 ($15,109) to date

Products
Programming and site feasibility studies

Built
No

Leverage: Strengthening Neighborhoods through Design

"Things happen because people believe they can ... the Collaborative's help supports the sense that things are possible—that there is an ally and resource available to let you dream."
—*Tracy Broyles, Executive Director of Spiral Q Puppet Theater*

Home sweet home: The puppets range from a few inches to twenty feet high; each has particular storage requirements. Since most performances are done off-site, a loading area needs to be directly accessible to the workshop and storage.

Collaboration

Big Puppets: Big Space

Spiral Q is an organization with a primary focus on promoting social justice, but it's also a hotbed of creativity; the staff and a crew of volunteers construct the puppets, hand-sew the costumes, screen-print its signage, and build its sets. The workshop space needs a wide variety of areas for each of these tasks. The group also hosts education and public outreach events on-site, and has its own library and museum.

A "test-fit" examined the group's current space needs and evaluated what kind of building could effectively be adapted for their use—an exercise that architects do routinely for clients in the private market, but nonprofit clients (let alone arts troupes) rarely have resources to invest in this kind of exploratory planning work.

As of June 2011, the Collaborative continues to evolve its work with Spiral Q to assist them in understanding and documenting their space needs as they plan for growth in a new location. This process helped the organization to identify and build awareness among its staff about what type of building can be adapted for their unique use—a design service that the Collaborative has found to be particularly well suited for a high-capacity organization like Spiral Q.

Inviting the Neighbors In:
Programs Employing People

Collaboration

After four decades of helping people with developmental disabilities, the social services agency Programs Employing People (PEP) wanted to enhance its program of enriching people's lives through vocational and social activities. But the space it occupies had created a sense of isolation from the community. The Collaborative worked with leadership to identify a series of simple facility improvements that would help build community not only among consumers of PEP services, but with the surrounding neighborhood as well.

Location
1200 South Broad St. (at Federal St.), Point Breeze neighborhood, Philadelphia

Services completed
2005

Client
Programs Employing People (PEP)

Volunteers
Joseph Salerno, AIA; Veronica Viggiano, AIA; Emma Johnson; Brian Wenrich

Hours donated (value)
2003: 45 ($5,100);
2005: 181 ($12,890)

Products
Feasibility study, conceptual design

Awards
First prize, Pennsylvania Horticultural Society's City Garden Contest, 2010

Built
2009

From foreboding to inviting:
PEP was eager to change the courtyard's eight-foot travertine wall and two-foot iron rail, topped with razor wire—a less-than-welcoming exterior for an organization that wanted to draw people in, not keep people out. Security was an issue, but bringing the garden out to the street was of greater importance—to bring goodwill to the neighborhood.

Leverage: Strengthening Neighborhoods through Design

107

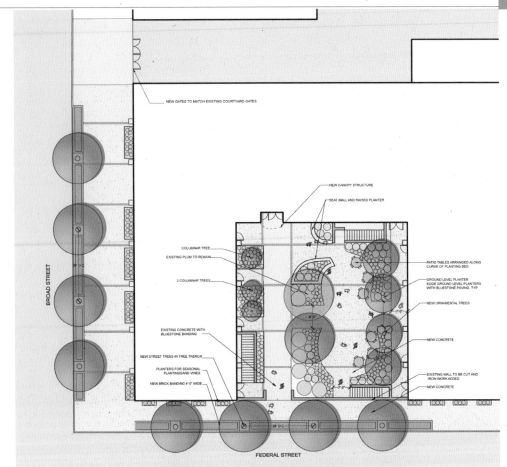

NEW GATES TO MATCH EXISTING COURTYARD GATES

NEW CANOPY STRUCTURE

SEAT WALL AND RAISED PLANTER

COLUMNAR TREE

EXISTING PLUM TO REMAIN

2 COLUMNAR TREES

PATIO TABLES ARRANGED ALONG
CURVE OF PLANTING BED

GROUND LEVEL PLANTER
EDGE GROUND LEVEL PLANTERS
WITH BLUESTONE PAVING, TYP

NEW ORNAMENTAL TREES

EXISTING CONCRETE WITH
BLUESTONE BANDING

NEW STREET TREES IN TREE TRENCH

PLANTERS FOR SEASONAL
PLANTINGS AND VINES

NEW BRICK BANDING 4'-0" WIDE

NEW CONCRETE

EXISTING WALL TO BE CUT AND
IRON WORK ADDED

NEW CONCRETE

BROAD STREET

FEDERAL STREET

28' O.C.

Starting Small

The Collaborative assisted with two projects to improve PEP's mid-century modern building at the corner of Broad (a major thoroughfare through South Philadelphia) and Federal Streets. The first was a modest warehouse project in 2003, which solidified the partnership. Then in 2005, a more extensive renovation focused on the generous courtyard and entryway formed by the C-shaped building, including aesthetic and functional improvements.

PEP needed dedicated storage to free up space within its on-site workshop, so the Collaborative's design team proposed creating a warehouse to occupy the side yard between PEP and the adjacent building. This was an efficient use of space, and the design team provided evaluations and proposals for the additional building as well as related zoning issues.

Spaces That Help People Flourish

One of the unique features of the existing space was a six-lane bowling alley—a holdover from the previous owners, the Sons of Italy social club—which PEP wanted to renovate for use with client activities. Affordable to maintain, the alley also had the potential to generate revenue if PEP opened it up to residents in the neighboring communities of Point Breeze and South Philadelphia.

The 2010 courtyard renovation enhanced outdoor seating and gardening opportunities, and created good will with the neighbors by extending activity out to the sidewalk. Now maintained with the help of PEP clients, the courtyard garden won first prize in the prestigious Pennsylvania Horticultural Society's City Garden Contest in 2010. PEP gains a third of its funding through contributions and fundraising, so a lovely, functional courtyard was a boon to a busy event season.

A garden atmosphere: Raised plant beds were relocated to allow for optimal circulation and seating, which were important given that the courtyard is a popular site for lunchtime breaks. In June 2011, PEP was pursuing the last phase of improvements, including planters along the sidewalk at the base of the building walls.

Beneficiaries of design: Executive Director Graham Gill (far left) with some of PEP's consumers.

Grim interiors: The well-kept Colonial Revival facade belied dim, outmoded spaces and drop ceilings inside.

Location
80 Windsor Ave., Narberth, Pennsylvania

Services completed
2004

Client
Narberth Community Library

Volunteers
Brawer & Hauptman Architects; CCM; Joe Matje; Nina Simonettiin

Hours donated (value)
236 ($26,730)

Sustainable design features
Energy-efficient heating, ventilation, and air conditioning system

Consultant for final design
Brawer & Hauptman Architects

Built
2007

An Update after Eighty Years:
Narberth Community Library

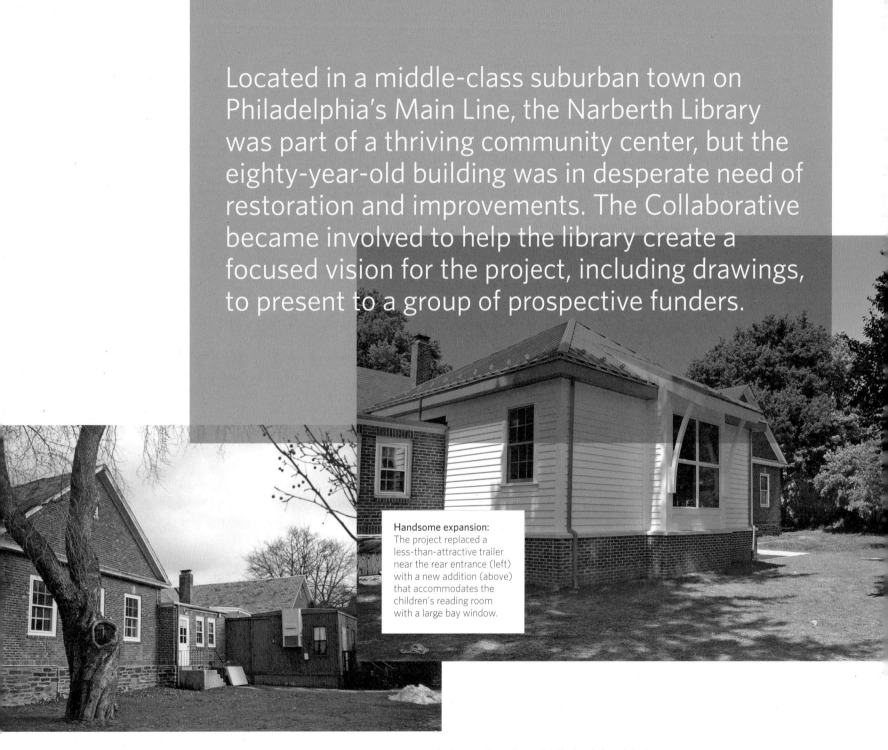

Located in a middle-class suburban town on Philadelphia's Main Line, the Narberth Library was part of a thriving community center, but the eighty-year-old building was in desperate need of restoration and improvements. The Collaborative became involved to help the library create a focused vision for the project, including drawings, to present to a group of prospective funders.

Handsome expansion:
The project replaced a less-than-attractive trailer near the rear entrance (left) with a new addition (above) that accommodates the children's reading room with a large bay window.

Step One: Create a Vision

The site also includes a playground and meeting spaces for the Girl Scout headquarters and the American Legion Hall. But the library's space needs had exceeded the building footprint, which meant spilling over into a less-than-attractive trailer attached near the library's rear entrance.

The Collaborative helped because the library lacked the funding to do even the basic design work needed to get the project underway. The Collaborative's building assessments and drawings enabled Narberth to secure the funding that ultimately paid for design development and construction.

The final project upgraded the facility to include energy-efficient heating and air conditioning, as well as ADA compliant restrooms, and upgraded lighting, smoke detection, and alarm systems. These bread-and-butter improvements gave the community the opportunity make the library more appealing and functional.

New heights: The dramatic double-height ceilings that had been hidden for thirty years by dropped ceiling tiles were revealed and complemented by state-of-the-art lighting.

North Elevation

Collaboration

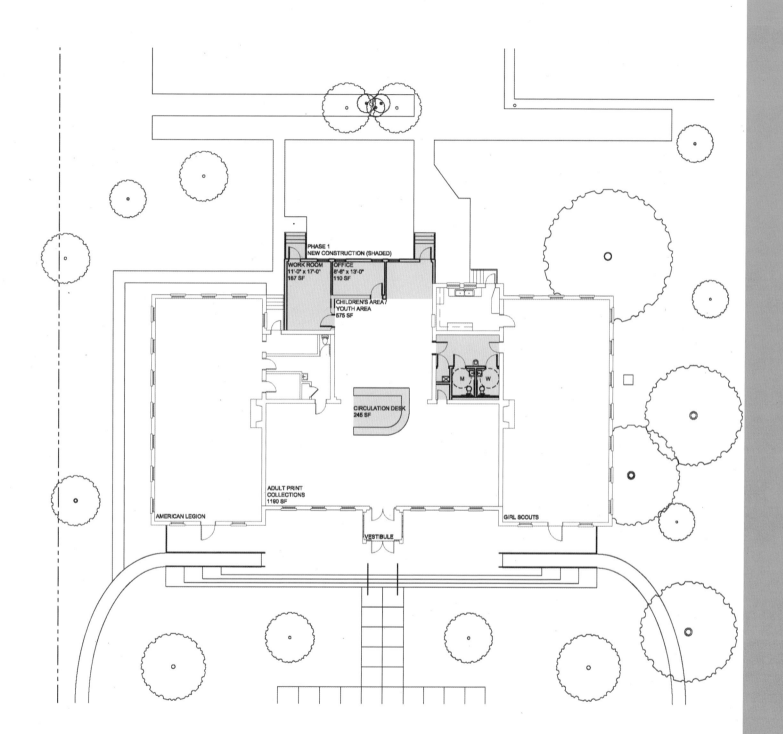

PHASE 1
NEW CONSTRUCTION (SHADED)

WORK ROOM
11'-0" x 17'-0"
187 SF

OFFICE
8'-6" x 13'-0"
110 SF

CHILDREN'S AREA /
YOUTH AREA
575 SF

M   W

CIRCULATION DESK
245 SF

ADULT PRINT
COLLECTIONS
1190 SF

AMERICAN LEGION

GIRL SCOUTS

VESTIBULE

North

Keeping the bays: The Collaborative's housing prototypes used the standard vocabulary of the row houses (bay windows, cornices, and zero setbacks) but also offered new amenities.

Building a Better Row House:
Allegheny West Foundation

Location
2800 block of Garnet St.;
1900 block of Somerset St.,
Allegheny West neighbor-
hood, Philadelphia

Services completed
2004

Client
Allegheny West Foundation

Volunteers
Francis Cauffman Foley
Hoffman, Architects, Ltd.

Hours donated (value)
484 ($36,070)

Products
Conceptual block and
site plans

Consultant for final design
CICADA Architecture/
Planning, Inc.; Blackney Hayes
Architects

Built
2004 to present

The Collaborative saw an opportunity to help the Allegheny West Foundation (AWF) devise some unconventional solutions to a common urban problem: filling in gaps between row houses on otherwise stable blocks. The approach required going beyond redeveloping single house lots; instead they sought to ask, "How can we combine two or three vacant lots or buildings to create a better row house?" The Collaborative responded with a variety of conceptual plans for AWF to use as prototypes.

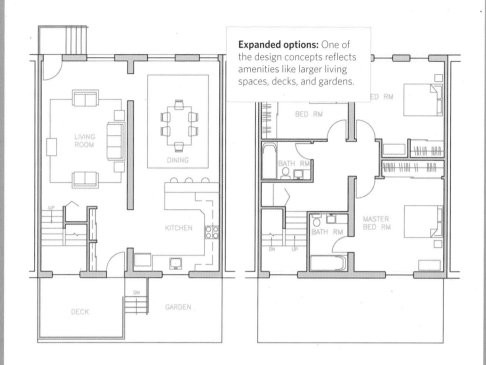

Expanded options: One of the design concepts reflects amenities like larger living spaces, decks, and gardens.

Rediscovering the "Forgotten Blocks"

AWF had a long track record of revitalizing this neighborhood, which lies in the shadow of the Hunting Park West industrial district. Since 2002, the area has been poised for new economic development, after suffering suburban flight, deindustrialization, and disinvestment. But some residents in one corner of Allegheny West felt overlooked. AWF saw promise in the "Forgotten Blocks," which were within walking distance of a growing mixed-use industrial district where new neighborhood-based jobs were anticipated.

Prototypes and Options

At the same time, AWF's strategy of targeting redevelopment to specific blocks was a new idea. Combining two vacant lots or a vacant house and lot to develop one larger house made them strong contenders for Philadelphia Redevelopment Authority funding. These two approaches distinguished AWF in the city's development landscape.

Design *Is the* Future

BY BRIAN PHILLIPS AND TODD WOODWARD

2011 MARKS TWENTY YEARS OF THE COMMUNITY DESIGN COLLABORATIVE— twenty years of service to nonprofit organizations, of connecting designers with volunteer opportunities, and of projects that, together, have raised the bar considerably for design in Philadelphia. This is certainly a cause for celebration, but it is also an opportunity to consider the future of the organization over the next twenty years. As architects and Collaborative volunteers, we are confident that the Collaborative will continue to promote change, foster innovative partnerships, create projects, and lead design professionals into new territory. The Collaborative could employ the skills of its volunteer design professionals and the expertise it has developed over time to address issues at a wide variety of scales and questions not traditionally considered design problems. This essay argues that, at this time in our history, the design field is charged with great transformative potential and that both the Collaborative and the design professions should support such transformation.

Design and designers have a significant role to play in the future of our cities and regions. Government officials and the business community would not have taken this statement seriously twenty years ago, when the Collaborative began providing pro bono design services to underserved organizations and neighborhoods. Throughout its history, and especially at the beginning, the Collaborative filled an important gap—one that spanned conventionally funded projects with high levels of support and projects that never materialized. This role came to be known as "community design," and later, more broadly as "public interest design." Typical project types included low- or mixed-income housing, public parks, school yards, and urban streetscapes: the kinds of buildings and spaces with which we interact on a daily basis in our communities. With this work, the Collaborative has championed the importance of participatory design efforts and the idea that every citizen deserves the benefits of a well-designed environment.

These types of projects will continue to be important to the Collaborative's mission as well as to the city at large. However, as we look toward the future of the organization, we must seek new gaps to fill and emerging issues that could significantly benefit from design resources. In its first twenty years, the Collaborative emphasized **community** by connecting design professionals to local mission-oriented groups, to explore projects that otherwise would not have happened. The organization encourages, actively arranges, and fosters **collaboration** throughout the development of each project— collaboration among all types of design professionals, as well as partnerships between neighbors, neighborhoods, and potential stakeholders. In a world characterized by intense new challenges and an increasing awareness of creativity as a productive tool for problem solving, the Collaborative should seek in the next phase of its work to push the limits of **design**.

new landscapes, or transformed commercial corridors, but include broader concerns such as public policy questions and social issues that are typically considered outside the realm of design thinking.

We see this emerging role of design—which allows thoughtful practitioners to solve problems and add value in pragmatic, high performance, and innovative ways—as integral to reflective design practice,[1] and also as a critical component to the improvement of our communities. Though it can be difficult to quantify certain benefits of design, the current climate requires that we channel more political, economic, and design energy into achieving measurable gains and replicable strategies. The Collaborative and other organizations like it should lead this effort, preparing and educating design professionals and community groups alike along the way.

Defining Design

The design challenges emerging in the twenty-first century are significantly different from those of the twentieth. With shifting and often unstable economic conditions, a worldwide explosion of urbanism, and widespread environmental issues, design is more important than ever. Historically, design has been viewed as merely an aesthetic exercise in which designers bring visual and experiential appeal to new and reused environments. We advocate instead for design as a problem-solving tool—a creative generator of high-impact, value-added solutions. Precedents for this thinking span from game theory and online user-generated content to Apple's comprehensive emphasis on design. Design should not be simply a reactive process, but rather an exercise in leadership, one that unlocks new potential on multiple scales for a better future.

What might this mean for the Collaborative? While the twenty-first century should be an exciting time for designers, given the potential to have broad and deep influence, our professions are not fully prepared to capitalize on this opportunity. Design professionals are taught and become skilled at how to imagine future possibilities that others may be unable to envision. These possibilities are not limited to renovated buildings,

A Seat at the Table

The Collaborative has been successful at increasing the profile of design and the design community relative to civic and urban policy issues that impact the built environment in Philadelphia. Though the organization initially worked along the margins of development activity in the city, the Collaborative has gradually become an established voice that represents the importance of quality design. This expertise would be useful to other cities, regions, and even countries that are in need of creative thinking regarding issues of the built environment.

Although politicians, economists, and business owners all participate from the beginning of a major planning effort, the reality is that architects and designers often do not. Brian recently led a studio at the University of Pennsylvania's School of Design (PennDesign) that focused on rebuilding in the wake of the 2010 earthquake in Haiti. The charge was to explore the role of the designer in the context of disaster relief and to consider how the students' design work could benefit the rebuilding effort. Though the group had done considerable research in advance of a trip to Haiti, they came to see that the challenges were not limited to destruction from the earthquake, as tragic and intense as it was. Many of the most serious problems grew out

local conditions and allow the organization to gain insight that in turn would benefit the work in Philadelphia? It is beyond the scope of this essay to answer such questions, but the Collaborative's track record over the past two decades suggests that they are worth serious consideration.

The Value of Design

Closer to home but with similarly broad relevance are questions of environmental responsibility, which provide an avenue for engagement that the Collaborative has not yet fully explored. Effectively addressing environmental issues requires transcending political boundaries, thinking creatively, and devising unique partnerships—activities at which the Collaborative already excels. Without treading into the territory of green building organizations, the Collaborative could investigate topics related to the intersection of built and natural environments on behalf of the community groups it serves. For example, as costs continue to rise, the large-scale need to generate energy in an environmentally responsible way will have implications for countless decisions in local planning as well as urban and regional design. At the scale of individual buildings, increasing energy costs will consume a greater proportion of building owners' budgets, and therefore provide incentive for building system upgrades that not only pay for themselves in the short term but also can offset the cost of other improvements. The cost of energy is sure to impact large and small nonprofits alike and change the nature of their potential building projects. The Collaborative is in a unique position to proactively address these issues.

Given the environmental and financial implications inherent in energy issues, the potential value—environmental, monetary, and otherwise—of thoughtful and critical design work could be significant. The value of design and design services, both in qualitative and quantitative terms, has always been among the key concerns of the Collaborative. However, it has been a challenge to communicate to those outside the organization the value of the projects it creates and the pro bono services it facilitates. This is, at least in part, because design professionals in general struggle to make the case for the value of their work.[2] Stakeholders regarded designers as expendable during the early planning for the future of Haiti, as have decision makers in the context of the recession. The consensus seems to be that, when the going gets tough, design is a luxury that we can all live without.

Is this because society simply does not understand the value of design? Or is it because architects and our colleagues fail to make the public aware of our capabilities? The design community may have become complacent during the economic expansion of the pre-recession years. For most architects and planners, work and design fees were plentiful; self-reflection

of the prevailing conditions that existed prior to the earthquake for many Haitians, given decades of political corruption, environmental degradation, and improper construction technology. The earthquake dramatically highlighted these underlying factors. The students came to understand the complex process of a major rebuilding strategy: the non-governmental organizations (NGOs), the myriad of committees, and the strategic (local and global) alliances. Though many other parties are at the planning table at the outset of such an effort, designers generally are not. It seems that architects are called to the table once a project is defined—and a request for proposals is ready to be issued. However, the thinking and decision-making that occurs prior to establishing a project are of crucial importance to the quality and relevance of what is actually designed and ultimately implemented. The Collaborative has already demonstrated the possibilities of an expansive role for the application of design to real, on-the-ground issues, and we think it should amplify this important mission. A critical advocacy role for the Collaborative moving forward could be to promote the role of designers as broad problem solvers and adept strategic thinkers.

Though it may initially seem unrelated, the comparison between rebuilding work in Haiti and the work of the Collaborative in Philadelphia is instructive and raises a series of questions about the role of the organization. As definitions of "community" evolve in our increasingly connected world, should the Collaborative's work expand to include regional or inter-city issues? Could teams of design professionals address issues of infrastructure, large-scale planning, or even transportation in ways that government agencies cannot? Are there places outside the Philadelphia area where the Collaborative's services and knowledge might both improve

Design *Is* the Future

Without losing the base of collaboration and the focus on community, could the next phase of the Collaborative's work push the limits of design?

seemed unnecessary in a booming economy. Now, as our economy recovers from the recent recession, it is clear that this will be a slow process. The next decade may be spent regaining lost economic ground. The outreach that the Collaborative undertakes on behalf of the design community and the projects that are created by its work are even more important during such times, to the design community and the general public alike.

There is much that all practicing design professionals might learn from the Collaborative and its approach to making design relevant to the broader community. The organization has already begun to tackle some of the issues that could make or break the design professions in the years to come. As designers, are we going to be stylists or strategists? Are we budget busters or are we clever with how to get the most for the minimum? Are we advocates for our own egos or advocates for a better future? With initiatives such as Infill Philadelphia, the Collaborative already addresses such questions, with promising outcomes.

Building on a Successful Model

We see great possibilities for the Collaborative to embrace and expand on the ideas embodied in Infill Philadelphia, a program in which the Collaborative identified and worked with local and regional partners to address significant urban issues in the context of design challenges around specific topics. In 2010, the topic for Infill Philadelphia was "Industrial Sites." Todd led a project by SMP Architects that considered how to encourage new types of industrial activity in the city. Entitled "Neighborhood Fabric(ation)," the project proposes individual and small-scale workshop spaces supported by shared services, including a membership-based advanced shop space and adjacent community and public uses (see left). The idea is that a mix of related uses could draw a range of people—residents, consumers, and

workers—to the site for a variety of reasons including jobs, retail, access to tools, and continuing education. Similar small-scale and individual production, combined with shared and community resources, could be replicated at other urban sites in Philadelphia and beyond. The details of this particular project, however, are less important than the idea that the act of design and the implementation of design thinking that the Collaborative champions yields strategies and opportunities that would not otherwise exist.

The future of the Collaborative should be to help reshape the role of the design community—in Philadelphia, certainly, but with wide-ranging implications. As with the organization's work to date, this reshaping would not come as a grand manifesto, but as the accumulation of a series of small, thoughtful moves. The first twenty years have provided a wealth of such incremental improvements, as this book documents. Architects, and design professionals more generally, can identify key challenges and serve as advocates for and agents of positive change. The Collaborative should continue to frame issues of importance and to advance the role of design in addressing these issues.

Opportunities abound for designers and design thinking to fill underlying gaps, though many of these may exist outside the typical understanding of what constitutes a design problem. The Collaborative should continue to emphasize design professional participation in the very early stages of planning, regardless of the scope of the undertaking, in order to increase the chances for the ultimate success of a project. As we continue to make predictions for the next twenty years, our core belief is that the Collaborative should unearth new territories for design energy—new project types, underserved constituencies, and innovative tactics. The Collaborative should ask tough questions to provoke and inspire government, institutions, and communities to face the difficult realities of the future with confidence and creativity.

1   We are using the term "reflective practice" in the context described by Donald Schon in *The Reflective Practitioner* (London: Temple Smith, 1983).
2   Recent economic conditions illustrate the issue of the perceived value of design work. Throughout the downturn, architects and other designers have been disproportionately out of work and, it would seem, under-valued. The construction industry as a whole was hurt badly by the recession and the architectural community was devastated, especially in certain urban areas.

BY BETH MILLER

An Overview of the Collaborative

The Community Design Collaborative works to strengthen neighborhoods in Philadelphia and beyond by coordinating pro bono design for nonprofits through a dedicated network of volunteer design professionals. Community design is an important part of the revitalization process and a critical element of livable, sustainable neighborhoods.

The Collaborative harnesses the urban energy, talents, and commitment of design professionals (architects, engineers, planners, landscape architects, estimators, and others), who work with energetic nonprofit, civic, and community leaders to envision a better future for citizens. The organization provides early feasibility studies and design services to nonprofits on site-specific projects, and develops model projects that promote dialogue and problem solving around critical issues in the city and region.

The Collaborative focuses on core issues affecting the quality of life in Philadelphia and surrounding counties such as housing, open space, commercial corridors, food access, and social services. Targeting direct services to community-serving nonprofits, the Collaborative works in the context of the built environment as just one aspect of the larger goal of revitalizing and strengthening communities.

Service Grants

Through responsive service grants, the Collaborative coordinates teams of volunteers from a range of design professions to bring a variety of skills to the table. Perhaps the most important skill we promote through our volunteer design professionals is problem solving. Our nonprofit clients face an all-too-common dilemma: while they have stellar track records in identifying needs and delivering programs and services, they seldom designate line items in their budgets to hire design professionals to help develop conceptual plans for capital improvements. We believe this preliminary aspect of planning is essential for effective, community-attentive design.

Combining design teams with nonprofits early in the process (what we call the first 10 percent or "pre-predevelopment") engages the power of design by unleashing possibilities, sparking reinvestment, and pushing the envelope for a brighter, more sustainable future. Meeting people where they are—offering design solutions that address issues of concern on their front stoop, on their block, or in their neighborhood—creates an undeniable connection between the design of the built and natural environments and the quality of life in their neighborhood.

The process of working with community groups and nonprofits on site-specific projects that excite them is what makes the Collaborative service grant model so unique. A community organization invites design teams to offer expertise and technical assistance that help put to paper its vision for a renewed facility or reactivated space. The final product, a bound report, helps the organization document and illustrate how these ideas can generate new anchors for a thriving neighborhood—places to gather, access services, and celebrate community.

This grassroots perspective makes the Collaborative unique among built-environment intermediaries in Philadelphia. The Collaborative serves as a matchmaker—connecting engaged community leaders with engaged design professionals who share passions for improving quality of life for all residents. Our volunteers have social justice in their blood. With leadership from a dedicated Board and a motivated Advisory Council, Collaborative staff coalesce the desire and skills of professionals who seek to deliver solutions to the communities they serve. The results are brick-and-mortar foundations for community, civic, and neighborhood pride.

We often say the process is as important—if not more important—as the products we provide. Working together helps groups weigh options, secure stakeholder buy-in, and secure the social fabric of neighborhoods while improving the quality of their built and natural environments. Community input, participation, and instigation are core values. Assisting civic and community organizations in testing the feasibility of community enhancement projects helps to strengthen the social fabric, which often underpins a thriving neighborhood in less-than-tangible ways.

Infill Philadelphia

Through Infill Philadelphia—a five-year, three-phase proactive initiative launched in 2005—the Collaborative cultivated partnerships with thought leaders to address design challenges related to advocacy. In the pilot phase, we teamed up with NeighborhoodsNow to address scattered and small-scale sites with potential for reuse as affordable housing. The results exceeded our expectations. Our service grant model was the foundation, but we added three service grants with promotion and packaging that took us to another level. The clear-eyed stewardship, expertise, and knowledge of our partners propelled us to consider the sum of the parts—to use design as a tool to advocate for policy and funding support.

With the support of the William Penn Foundation, the Collaborative used this model to establish Infill Philadelphia. We partnered with the Philadelphia office of the Local Initiatives Support Corporation to craft a design challenge to address commercial corridors in phase one. For phase two, we addressed design challenges related to food access in partnership with the Reinvestment Fund and the Food Trust and with support from Pennsylvania's Fresh Food Financing Initiative. We recently completed work with the Philadelphia Industrial Development Corporation to explore industrial reuse, with support from the Urban Land Institute Philadelphia District Council.

Each phase of Infill has expanded the conversation using design as a tool to address intractable urban problems. Through this series of design challenges, the Collaborative has tapped into local expertise, partnering with thought leaders to help reposition critical issues and unleash the possibilities for reinvestment, civic engagement, and neighborhood-based community revitalization in an unapologetically urban way.

Looking Ahead

The Collaborative has a strong platform on which to build our future. We will continue to use design as a catalyst to ask provocative questions, encourage innovative thinking, and provide pragmatic, practical solutions for urban design challenges. We will create more partnerships and inspire new spirited public discussions among residents, policy makers, investors, designers, business owners, and developers. We will continue to rely upon the urban energy of our interdisciplinary volunteers and nonprofit leaders to leverage resources, attention, and action to strengthen neighborhoods through design, one project at a time.

The Collaborative Community

CLIENTS, VOLUNTEERS (SINCE 2001), AND PARTNERS

Clients

ACHIEVEability • ACORN Housing Corporation of PA • Advocacy for Health Education Awareness and Development • Advocate Community Development Corporation • The African American Museum in Philadelphia • African Cultural Alliance of North America, Inc. • AIA Philadelphia • AIDS Care Group • Aldersgate Youth Service Bureau • All Saints Parish Rhawnhurst • Allegheny West Foundation • American Street Corridor Business Association • Arch Street United Methodist Church • Asian Arts Initiative • Asociación de Puertorriqueños en Marcha, Inc. • Bache-Martin Home & School Association • Belmont Village Community Association • Benefits Data Trust • Bethel Holy Temple Church • Beulah Baptist Church • Big Brothers Big Sisters SE Pennsylvania • Books Through Bars • Borough of Millbourne • Boxing Association of America, Inc. • BuildaBridge International • Byron Story Youth Restoration Career Center • Calcutta House • Calvin Presbyterian Church • Cambodian Association of Greater Philadelphia • Caring About Sharing, Inc. • Carousel at Pottstown, Inc. • Carroll Park Community Council • Cedar Park Neighbors • Celestial Church of Christ • Center City Proprietors Association • Center for Architecture • Center for Literacy • Central Germantown Council • Central Montgomery MH/MR Center • Centro Nueva Creacion • Chester's Community Grocery Co-op • Chinatown Building and Education Foundation • The Church Down the Way • Citizens for the Restoration of Historic LaMott • City of Philadelphia Department of Commerce • City Parks Association • City Year Greater Philadelphia • The Clay Studio • Community Education Center • Community Legal Services of Philadelphia • Congregation of Vilna • Cook-Wissahickon Home & School Association/Cook Wissahickon Green Committee • Cramer Hill Community Development Corporation • Cranaleith Spiritual Center • C. W. Henry School Home and School Association • Darby Library Company • Delaware Valley Association for the Education of Young Children • Design Corps • Dignity Housing • Earth Rights Institute • East Parkside Residents' Association • East Passyunk Avenue Business Improvement District • Empowerment Group • Energy Coordinating Agency of Philadelphia, Inc. • The Enterprise Center Community Development Corporation • Face to Face at St. Vincent's • Fairmount Community Development Corporation • Fairmount Park Art Association • Fellowship Farm • First African Baptist Church of Philadelphia • First Baptist Church of Paschall, Inc. • Frankford Community Development Corporation • Frankford Friends School • The Frankford Group Ministry • The Franklin Concept Group, Inc. • Friends General Conference • Friends of Cianfrani Park • Friends of Dickinson Square • Friends of Gold Star Park • Friends of Hart Park • Friends of Marconi Plaza • Friends of Peace Valley Nature Center, Inc. • Friends of Powers Park • Friends of Pretzel Park • Friends of Ridley Creek State Park • Friends of Schuylkill River Park • Friends of Seger Park Playground • Friends of the Inn Yard Park • Friends of the Santore Library • Friends of Weccacoe Playground • George W. Nebinger Elementary School • Girard Coalition, Inc. • Gold Medal Karate Inc. • Grace Baptist Church of Germantown • Grace Church and the Incarnation • Greater Philadelphia Food Bank • Green Village Philadelphia • Greene Street Friends School • Greenfield Home & School Association • Habitat for Humanity Germantown • Habitat for Humanity Philadelphia • HealthLink Medical Center • Hispanic Association of Contractors & Enterprises • HomeWorks • Impact Services Corporation • Impacting Your World CDC • Inter-Community Development Corporation • Intercultural Family Services • J. R. Masterman Home & School Association • JASTECH Development Services, Inc. • John H. Taggart Elementary School • Kelsey G. Keeys CDC • Lansdowne Economic Development Corporation • Legal Aid of Southeastern Pennsylvania • Lemon Ridge Garden, Inc. • Liberian Association of Pennsylvania, Inc. • Libertae, Inc. • Liberty Resources, Inc. • The Lighthouse • Lincoln Day Nursery • Logan Community Development Corporation • LOGAN Hope • Lois' Learning Tree Daycare Center • Lutheran Settlement House • Macedonia Family Development and Learning Center • Manayunk Development Corporation • Manna on Main Street • Mariposa Inc. • Mayfair Community Development Corporation • Meadowood • Meredith Home & School Association • Metropolitan Baptist Church • Minority Arts Resource Council, Inc. • The Miquon School • Mizpah Seventh-Day Adventist Church • Morton Station Preservation Committee • Mount Hope Baptist Church • Mount Zion CDC • Mt. Airy Learning Tree • Mt. Airy Presbyterian Church • Mt. Airy USA • Mt. Sinai Stretch the Limits • Mt. Tabor Community Education & Economic • Development Corporation (CEED) • Narberth Community Library • Neighborhood Gardens Association • Neighborhood Interfaith Movement • NeighborhoodsNow • Neighbor to Neighbor CDC • New Frankford Community Y • New Hope Freewill Baptist Church • New Jerusalem Laura • New Kensington CDC • Nicetown Community Development Corporation • Norris Square Civic Association • Norris Square Neighborhood Project • North Light Community Center • North Penn Civic Association • North Philadelphia Community Help, Inc. • Northern Home for Children • Northwest Counseling Service, Inc. • Northwestern Stables, Inc. • Nueva Esperanza, Inc. • Oak Lane Tree Tenders • Ogontz Avenue Revitalization Corporation • Old Pine Community Center • Open Arms Against Abuse Services, Inc. • Open Borders Project • The Other Side, Inc. • Overbrook Farms Civic Foundation/Overbrook Farms Club • Overbrook Presbyterian Church • Parkside Historic Preservation Corporation • The Partnership CDC • Pennhurst Memorial & Preservation Alliance • Pennypack Farm Education Center for • Sustainable Food Systems • People Achieving Positive Attitudes • People's Community Center • People's Emergency Center • Philadelphia Art Alliance • Philadelphia Association of Community • Development Corporations • Philadelphia Boys Choir • Philadelphia Children's Alliance • Philadelphia Chinatown Development Corporation • Philadelphia Community Arts Network • Philadelphia Doll Museum • Philadelphia Economic Revitalization Corporation • Philadelphia Education Fund • Philadelphia Folklore Project • Philadelphia Group Mental Health Association • Philadelphia Industrial Development Corporation • Philadelphia Mural Arts Advocates • Philadelphia Neighborhood Housing Services • Philadelphia Physicians for Social Responsibility • Philadelphia Rooftop Farm (PRooF) • Philadelphia Society for Services to Children • Philadelphia Volunteer Lawyers for the Arts • Philadelphia Youth Network • Pleasantview Baptist Church • Point Breeze Civic Association • Pottstown Area Police Athletic League • Powelton Village Civic Association • The Preschool Project • Preservation Alliance of Greater Philadelphia • The Print Center • Programs Employing People • Project H.O.M.E. • Protestant Advisory Board at Temple University • Rebuilding Together • Refuge for the Perishing Holy Temple • Resurrection Baptist Church CDC • River Crossing Community Church • Roxborough Development Corporation • S. Weir Mitchell Elementary School • Samuel S. Fleisher Art Memorial • Seger Park Dog Owner's Association • SHARE Food Program, Inc. • SILOAM • SOSNA • South Broad Street Neighborhood Association • South Philadelphia H.O.M.E.S. Inc. • Southwest Community Development Corporation • Southwest Philadelphia Seventh-Day Adventist Church • Spiral Q Puppet Theater • Spirit and Truth Fellowship • St. Mark Outreach Baptist Church • St. Mary's Episcopal Church, Hamilton Village • St. Peter's Episcopal Church • Swarthmore Centennial Foundation (SCF) • Swarthmore Town Center • Tabor Children's House • Taney Youth Baseball Association • Tate, White & Smith Assoc. for Community Dev., Inc • Temple Brotherhood Mission Ministries • Tioga United • Trane Stop Resource Institute, Inc. • 29th Street CDC • UC Green • United American Indians of the Delaware Valley • University City Historical Society • Urban Hope Training Center • Visitation BVM School • Wallingford Presbyterian Church • Waters Memorial Community Center • Weavers Way Community Programs • West Philadelphia Child Care Network • William Way Community Center • Wissahickon Neighbors Civic Association • Women Against Abuse, Inc. • Women's Community Revitalization Project • Word Tabernacle Baptist Church • Wynnefield Heights Civic Association, Inc. • Wynnefield Overbrook Revitalization Corporation • YWCA of Germantown

Firm Volunteers

About Face Type & Design • Abriola Company • Advanced Foodservice Solutions • AK Architecture, LLC • Alderson Engineering, Inc. • Always by Design • Andrea Daniels Planning and Interior Design • The Atlantic Group • Austin + Mergold LLC • Ballinger • BEAM, ltd.

• Becker & Frondorf • Bench Dog Design • Bernardon Haber Holloway Architects, PC • Birdsall Services Group • Bittenbender Construction, LP • BLT Architects • Bohlin Cywinski Jackson • Brands Imaging • Brandt + Ginder Architecture Inc. • Brawer & Hauptman Architects • Brett Webber Architects PC • Brian Szymanik Architects • Brown & Keener • Bruce E. Brooks & Associates • Buell Kratzer Powell Ltd. • Burns Morrissey Architecture + Design LLP • Burt Hill • BWA architecture + planning • Casaccio Architects • CCM • CDA & I Architecture and Interiors, Ltd. • Cecil Baker & Partners • Center City District • Charles A. Evers, AIA Architecture & Preservation • Charles Loomis Chariss McAfee Architects • Cherry Hill Township Community Dev. Dept. • CHPlanning, Ltd.-Delaware County• Christopher Allen Landscape Architecture • CICADA Architecture/ Planning, Inc. • City of Philadelphia Office of Housing and Community Development • CLR Design, Inc. • CMX • Conley Design, Inc. • Construction Management Solution • Constructure Management, Inc. • Continuum Architecture & Design • Cooke Brown LLC • Core Management, Inc. • CVM Engineers • DataFac Inc. Architects • Davis Langdon • DB-3D • DeHaven Templeton • Diana T. Myers and Associates • DIE Creative • DIGSAU Architecture/ Urbanism • D'Lauro & Rodgers • DLR Group/Becker Winston • Domus, Inc. • Duffield Associates, Inc. • E. Allen Reeves, Inc. • Econsult Corporation • Elwell Studio • Energy Coordinating Agency of Philadelphia, Inc. • The Enterprise Center • Ewing Cole • F. X. Browne, Inc. • Fairmount Park Art Association • Firmarchitecture • Flatiron Building Company • Floss Barber, Inc. • Francis Cauffman • Friday Architects/Planners Inc. • Gardner Fox Associates • Gilbane Building Company • Gilmore & Associates, Inc. (Chester County Office) • Gray Smith's Office • Grenald Waldron Associates • Group Melvin Design • GYA Architects, Inc. • The Harman Group • Hellyer Berman Lewis, Inc. • Hessert Construction • Hierarchy Golf Design • HK Lighting Design Inc • Hollister Construction Services • Hunter Landscape Design • Hunter Roberts Construction Group • Interface Studio • Interface Studio Architects, LLC • International Consultants, Inc. • Jacobs/Wyper Architects • James Wentling/ Architects • Jibe Design • JKR Partners LLC • John Hubert Architects • John Milner Architects, Inc. • Jonathan Alderson Landscape Architects, Inc. • JxN Studio LLC • Keast & Hood Co. • KieranTimberlake Associates, LLP • Kimmel Bogrette Architecture + Site, Inc. • Kitchen &

Associates Architectural Services, PA • KlingStubbins • KMS Design Group LLC • Kramer/Marks Architects • KSK Architects Planners Historians, Inc. • KSS Architects LLP • Lager Raabe Skafte Landscape Architects, Inc. • Langan Engineering & Environmental Services, Inc. • Larsen & Landis • Lenhardt & Rodgers Architects • Levine & Company, Inc. • Lighthouse Architecture, Inc. • The Lighting Practice • Local Initiatives Support Corporation - Philadelphia • m2 Architecture • MacIntosh Engineering • MaGrann Associates • manifest AD • Marvin Waxman Consulting Engineers • Mary Ann Duffy Architect • Matthew Davis Landscape Design and Planning • McGillin Architecture, Inc. • Meliora Environmental Design LLC • MetEast High School • MGA Partners, Architects • Michelle Robinson Architects • Montgomery County Planning Commission • Moore Engineering Company • Moto DesignShop Inc. • Murray Construction • Nason Construction, Inc. • National Park Service • Numerof Construction Services, Inc. • OLIN • 119 degrees architects • Owner's Rep Inc. • Patriot Construction, Inc. • Penn Lighting Associates • Pennsylvania Horticultural Society • Philadelphia Corporation for Aging • Philadelphia Water Department • Pixelcraft Inc. • point line space • Pollio Associates, LLC • Premier Building Restoration, Inc. • Preservation Alliance of Greater Philadelphia • Ramla Benaissa Architects, LLC • RAM-Tech Engineers, Inc. • Resource Partnership • Re:Vision Architecture • Roland Noreika Architect • Roofmeadow • SALT Design Studio • sfs office design, llc • Shift Space Design LLC • SITE Landscape Architecture • Sky Architects • SMP Architects • Stuart G. Rosenberg Architects, P.C. • Studio Agoos Lovera • Studio Bryan Hanes • Studio Gaea • StudioJAED • STV Inc. • Synterra, Ltd. • Terra Studio • ThinkGreen LLC • Thomas A. Monari, PE • Thomas C. Faranda, P.E. • Thomas Comitta Associates, Inc. • Thornton Tomasetti • Tim Sienold 3D Artist/Animator • Torcon, Inc. • TRC Companies, Inc. • Turner Construction Company • UCI Architects, Inc. • University of Pennsylvania, Facilities & Real Estate Services • University of Pennsylvania, Urban Studies Program • Urban Engineers, Inc. • Urban Partners • U.S. General Services Administration • Viridian Landscape Studio • Wallace Roberts & Todd, LLC • Wesley Wei Architects • Wilson Consulting, Inc. • Z&F Consulting • Zimmerman Studio LLC

Individual Volunteers

Joe Abriola • Arthur Adams • Brittany Adams • Michele Adams • Ferdinand Addo • Katie Adema • Ted Agoos • Jai Agrawal • Joanne Aitken • Senemeh Akwei • Jonathan Alderson • Travis Alderson • Christopher Allen • Andy Allwine • Dustin Almon • Jaquelin Anderson • Kelly Anderson • Peter Anderson • Carl Andresen • Melissa Andrews • Marguerite Anglin • Toufik Aouiz • Jay Appleton • Laura Arahmjian • Allison Ardire • Billy Arias • Anthony Armento • Michael Armento • Lisa Armstrong • David Artman • Amma Asamoah • Mark Asher • Jason Austin • Rocco Avallone • Jeremy Avellino • Geraldo Aviles • Erick Bach • Prajakta Bagul • Joanna Baker • Patrick Baker • Cassandra Ballew • Christine Barbieri • Michelle Barbieri • Edward Barnhart • Jordan Barr • Monica Barton • Suzanna Barucco • Nancy Bastian • Jody Beck • Richard Beck • Bill Becker • James Behler • Ramla Benaissa • Michael Bennett • Barbara Benvenuti • Alice Berman • Bob Betsch • Kerri Bizzell • Laura Black • Laura Blackstone • Carolyn Blackwell • Michael Blumenthal • Wanda Bobonis • David Boelker • Jim Bogrette • Jana Booth • Mitch Bormack • Daniel Bosin • Casey Boss • Alexa Bosse • Lauren Bostic • John Bower • Taylor Boyd • Anthony Bracali • Jessica Brams-Miller • Brett Brand • Suzanne Brandt • David Brawer • Joseph Bray • Charles Brenton • Todd Bressi • Katie Broh • Jean-Pierre Brokken • Jeb Brookman • Kate Brower • Daniel Brown • David Brown • Derek Brown • Jessica Brown • Nancy Brown • Peter Brown • Ray Brown • Jeffrey Brummer • Gabrielle Bucak • Oscar Bujosa • Anthony Buonomo • Jillian Burgess • James Burke • Andrew Burkert • Christopher Burkett • Jack Burns • Thomas Burns • James Bush • Julie Bush • Jonathan Bykowski • Betsy Caesar • Vincent Calabro • Nicholas Calcagni • Chris Calemmo • Peter Camburn • Giovanni Caputo • Adam Carangi • Anthony Carango • Todd Carll • David Carlson • Sara Carlson • Anneliza Carmalt • Chad Carnahan • Donna Carney • Roberto Carretero • Christina Carter • Peggy Carter • Jason Causton • Gabriela Cesarino • Jane Cespuglio • Bruce Chamberlin • Alex Chan • Wandy Chang • Scott Chastain • Amy Chen • Yun-shang Chiou • Laine Cidlowski • Angela Cirino • Karen Clancy • James Coburn • Mark Coggin • Tracey Cohen • John Colarelli • Morton Collier • Tom Comitta • Roy Conard • Glen Conley • Leesa Conley • Katherine Coonradt • Makella Craelius • Richard Craig • Ben Cromie • Andrew Cronin • Martha Cross • Jason Crow • Erin Crowe • Bradford Crowley • Thomas Crowley • Christine Miller Cruiess • Jim Curry • Andrew Curtis • Jason Curtis • Chris Custren • Alexander Cutrona • Tara Cwitkowitz • Kate Czembor • Martin Dahmm • Rori Dajao • Scott Dalinka • John Dallinga • Kevin Dalton • Joseph D'Alu • Joshua Daniel • Andrea Daniels • David Daniels • Amrita Dasgupta • Angel Davis • Mathew Davis • Suzanne Dean • Gary Debes • Chris DeBruyn • Robert Decesari • Jeanna DeFazio Ventura • Gerald (Jay) DeFelicis • Robert DeHaven • Mary DeNadai • Cecelia Denegre • Peter Denitz • Danielle Denk • Harsha Desai • James De Stefano • Andrea DeVico • Liezl Diaz • Helen Diemer • Patricia DiFalco • Michael Digiacomo • Justin Diles • Ted Dillon • Daniel DiMucci • Jules Dingle • Ann Dinh • Justin DiPietro • Jeff Di Romaldo • Scott Dismukes • Julie Disston • Tavis Dockwiller • Felicia Doggell • Howard Dorf • Jennifer Dorr • Nathan Dort • Kim Douglas • Dan Driskell • Angelo Drummond • Elisabeth Dubin • Mary Ann Duffy • Cynthia Dukes • Alex Dunham • Terra Edenhart-Pepe • Susan Edens • Allison Edmonds • Christopher Edwards • Daryn Edwards • John Egan • Nissa Eisenberg • David Elliott • Maria Elosua • Jason Elwell • Carl Emberger • Sarah Endriss • Charles Evers • Suzanna Fabry • Jeff Fama • Tom Faranda • Amee Farrell • Eric Farrell • Susan Feenan • Illissa Figueroa • Adrian Fine • Emily Finigan • Barry Finkelstein • John Finley • Ian Fishman • Megan Fitzpatrick • Rob Fleming • Amy Floresta • Brian Flynn • Pat Foanio • Brian Ford • Julie Forejt • Jesse Forrester • Erin Fox • Mary Frazier • Andrea Frey • John Frondorf • Michael Funk • John Gallery • Brook Gardner • Dan Garofalo • James Gartside • Emmanuel Gee • David Gehringer • Mario Gentile • Rebecca Gentino • Elise Geyelin • Paula Giantsios • John Gibbons • Jackie Gibson • Jennifer Gibson • Stephen Gibson • Shaun Gilbert • Barry Ginder • Michael Gioffre • Stephen Giorgio • Sarah Gittens • Rachel Goffe • Jeff Goldstein • Mauricio Gomez • David Goodling • Robert Gould • Shashi Goyal • Laura Grant • Robert Green • Lee Greenwood • Stephen Greulich • Christina Grimes • Nicholas Groch • Gerard Gruber • Geoff Grummon • Allen Guenthner • Christina Guerrero • David Guinn • Jackie Gusic • Miriam Gutierrez-Cervantes • Kristen Haaf • Kara Haggarty • Kate Hallinan • Tom Halliwell • Norman Halloway • James Hammond • Lisa McDonald Hanes • Joseph Hang • Erin Hannegan • Micah Hanson • Mami Hara • Raven Hardison • Anne Harnish • Kersten Harries • David Harrower • Gregory Hart • Mike Hauptman • Christopher Heaven • Eric Heidel • Gregory Heller • Timothy Hemsath • Abigail Henry • Shanna Hensler-McDonald • Matt Herman • Brenna Herpmann • Kerry Herr • Jason Hill • Ryan Hill • David Hincher • David Hitt • John Hodos • Altje Hoekstra • Kenneth Hoffman • Patrick Hoffman • Tyrone Hofmann • David Hofmeister • Mary Holland • Myron Holowczak • Nicholas Holz • Nathan Hommel • Joseph Horan • Lori Horton • Tobiah Horton • Naquib Hossain • Nicole Hostettler • Robert Hotes • Theresa Houpt • Larry Houstoun • Leigh Howard • Jon Hoyle • Clifton Hubbard • John Hubert • Mathew Huffman • Mary Anne Hunter • Jennifer Hurley • Joyce Hwang • Anna Ishii • Michael Izzo • Stephen Jack • Ahmed Jama • Anthony James • Katie James • Verna James • Jack Jamison • John Janda • Joshua Janisak • Adam Jeckel • William Jelen • Satyendra Jenamani • Chris Jensen • Melissa Jest • Aaron Jezzi • Alisa Joe • Emma Johnson • Lou Johnson • Marcus Johnson • Peter Johnson • Sterling Johnson • Amy Jones • Britton Jones • Mary Judy • Molly Julian • Uk Jung • Raheen Kahn • Scott Kalner • David Kane • Paul Kangas-Miller • David Kanthor • Kenneth Kauffman • Janna Kauss • Nicole Keegan • Mark Keener • Kristin Keilt • Erin Keith • Carl Kelemen • Joshua Kelly • Scott Kelly • Tim Kerner • Danielle Kim • Richard King • Thomas Kirchner • Vera Kiselev • Susan Klein • Bodhi Knott • Caleb Knutson • Juliet Koczak • George Koenig • Robin Komita • Magdalena Kosz-Koszewska • Andrew Kraetzer • Darrell Kratzer • Richard Krause • Adam Krom • A. Richard Kron • Steve Krumenacker • Brian Kuhns • Aparna Kumar • Isaac Kwon • Richard Kydd • Anita Lager • Jigna Lagin • Brad Landis • Clayton Lane • Amanda Langweil • Elizabeth Lankenau • Holly Lanutti • Scott Larkin • Eric Larsen • Courtney LaRuffa • Erin Lauer • Andrew Lavine • Jill Lavine • Eddie Layton • Brian Leach • Larry Leary • Josh Leaskey • Howard Lebold • Danielle Lee • Juliet Lee • Trevor Lee • Joyce Lenhardt • Kathy Lent • Saramari Leon • Lotus Leong • Bonnie Leung • Nicole Levari • Sean Levengood • Jeffrey Levine • Peter Levins • Vibeke Lichten • Rachel Lijana • Jeffrey Linneman • Snezana Litvinovic • Pam Liu • Yan Liu • Don Lodge • Michael LoFurno • Donald Logan • Charles Loges • Vince Lombardi • Jenny Long • Charles Loomis • Diane Luckman • William Lukens • Robert Lundgren • Edward Lupinek • Xiaofeng Ma • Maria MacLaury • Sharon Maclean • Ashley Magloire • Natalie Malawey-Ednie • Robert Maloney • Rosa Mannion • Sephlyn Marcano • Christine Marsal • David

Marsh • Mayva Marshall-Moreno • William Marston • Jennifer Martel • Michael Martella • Caitlin Martin • Katy Martin • Muscoe Martin • Andrea Marzolf • Katie Masi • Joseph Matje • Ron Matson • Julia Matteo • Don Matzkin • Missy Maxwell • Chariss McAfee • George McCallister • Lisa McCann • Aran McCarthy • Jessica McCollum • Tom McCreesh • Megan McGinley • Charles McGloughlin • Ryan McGrath • Catherine McGuckin • Brad McGuirt • Carmen McKee • Michael McKeever • Marissa McMurtrie • Scott McNallan • Emily McNally • Dan Meier • John Mellett • William Mellix • Virginia Melnyk • Kira Merdiushev • Brian Merritt • Christopher Methven • Sean Metrick • Nando Micale • Aaron Miller • Ari Miller • Robin Miller • John Mixon • Charles Moleski • Erin Monaghan • Kevin Monaghan • Tom Monari • Adam Montalbano • Melissa Montgomery • Richard Moretti • Nathan Morgan • Karin Morris • James Morrissey • Rae Munroe • Linda Muronda • Jenna Murphy • Leah Murphy • Christiane Murray • Adam Musante • Nicholas Musser • Michael Nairn • Narintorn Narisaranukul • Tom Nason • Charles Nawoj • Nicole Neder • Amanda Neuenfeldt • Pamela Newman • Rashida Ng • Chi Nguyen • Benjamin Nia • Khephra Nielsen • Eric Nogami • Roland Noreika • Leslie Norvell • Sid Numerof • Susan Nurge • Christine O'Brien • Kenneth O'Brien • Michael Oei • Ian Optenberg • Charlie Oropallo • Jennifer Orr • Joshua Otto • Scott Page • Stephanie Palmer • Sylvia Palms • Evangelos Pappas • Mark Paronish • Julie Parrett • Shaun Patchell • Sneha Patel • Mark Paul • Michael Paul • Rachel Peiffer • Matthew Perna • Douglas Perry • Teisha Perry • Maarten Pesch • Jeff Peters • Karl Peters • Creola Petrescu • Brian Phillips • Jeremy Philo • Danielle Pizzutillio • Galen Plona • Julie Poeschel • Michele Pollio • Peter Porretta • Van Potteiger • Daniel Powell • Joseph Powell • Erin Powers • Steve Preiss • Jonathan Price • Michael Prifti • Bogna Pro • Joseph Pro • Lynn Przywara • Chris Pugliese • Joseph Pung • Nancy Putnam • David Quadrini • Linda Quinlan • Elizabeth Rairigh • Brad Randall • Jane Rath • Heather Raylinsky • Donald Raymond • Kurt Raymond • Laura Raymond • Veena Reddy • Colin Reed • Jamie Reeves • Robert Reeves • Julie Regnier • Sally Reynolds • Anthony Ricciardi • Robin Rick • Gavin Riggall • Scott Ritchie • Erin Roark • Richard Roark • Doug Robbins • Gaylen Roberts • Kevin Roberts • Edward Robinson • Judy Robinson • Michelle Robinson • Sophie Robitaille • Aaron Roche • Michael Roden • Anne Roderer • John Romano • Omar Rosa • Patrick Rose • Eli Rosen • Elaine Rosenberg-Cotton • Christine Rossi • Nicole Rossi • Chris Rouse • Rachel Royer • Laura Rozumalski • Kate Rutledge • Susan Ryan • Stephanie Saile • Joe Salerno • Lori Salganicoff • Eric Sallee • Paul Samala • Benjamin Samberg • Scott Sampson • James Sanderson • Mark Sanderson • Melissa Santos • Stephanie Sarin • Steve Saxon • Deborah Schaaf • Beth Schaffer • Marisa Schaffer • Tess Schiavone • David Schmidt • Michelle Schmitt • Anna Schmitz • Heather Schneider • Stephen Schoch • Steffi Schueppel • Sara Pevaroff Schuh • Rob Schultz • David Schweim • Clifford Schwinger • John Sciotto • Adam Scott • Annie Scott • David Seace • Kevin Selger • Leah Selkowitz • Ari Seraphin • Arundhati Sett • Kaushambi Shah • Robert Shamble • Ian Shao • Dean Sherwin • Morgan Shinsec • Robert Shoaff • Nirati Shukla • Michelle Shuman • Tim Sienold • Mark Silks • Chris Silver • Justin Silverthorn • Maki Silverthorn • Keith Simon • Nina Simonetti • Karen Skafte • Gray Smith • Gregory Smith • Kristen Smith • Sabra Smith • Susan Smith • Chris Soffientini • Devinder Soin • Jason Solinsky • Michael Spain • David Spangler • Michael Sparks • Jayne Spector • Kira Springart • Kwatee Stamm • Davin Stamp • Daniel Stanislaw • Samirah Steinmeyer • Michael Stern • Zachary Stevenson • Sydney Stewart • Sam Stewart-Haleion • Marcella Stokes • Edward Strockbine • Christopher Stromberg • Emily Stromberg • Jan Strouse • Patrick Stuart • Daniel Sullivan • Jennifer Summers • Dana Sunshine • Adam Supplee • John Suter • Anna Swanberg • Mitchell Swann • George Swisher • Brian Szymanik • Mike Tahara • Robin Tama • Lynne Templeton • Aleksandra Teresiak • Ashima Thakur • John Theobald • Todd Thomas • Denise Thompson • Jeanne Thompson • Keinan Thompson • Roxi Thoren • Karena Thurston • Brian Tiede • Kelly Tigera • Justin Tocci • Erika Tokarz • Robert Toomer • Sheena Toomey • Pete Torino • Kelly Tornes • Scott Torr • Roman Torres • Joshua Toth • Andy Toy • Jennifer Toy • Rick Tralies • Vasiliki Tsiouma • Kevin Turk • Lauren Ulmer • Jamie Unkefer • Thecla Uriyo • Rafael Utrera • Whitney Van Dean • Gary Van Vliet • Irene Vance • Ariel Vazquez • Anthony Venella • Ramnath Venkat • Joe Vetrano • Peter Vieira • Alexa Viets • Rebecca Vieyra • Veronica Viggiano • Frank Vinceguerra • Suzann Vogel • Alexandra Vondeling • Andrew Wagner • Scott Wagner • Matthew Wanamaker • Fon Wang • Natalie Wang • Larry Wapnitsky • Jim Ward • Mark Washington • Marvin Waxman • Brett Webber • Lynda Weber • Yu-Hua Wei • Jonathan Weiss • Rebecca Weiss • Brian Wenrich • Jim Wentling • Glenn Werner • Kristi Wescott • Juliet Whelan • William Whelan • Thomas Wiedenman • Car Wightman • Brian Wiginton • Alexander Will • Joshua Williams • Warren Williams • Heather Williams Hubert • Gregory Wilson • Jeff Wilson • Jane Winkel • Richard Winston • Aleksandra Wolchasty • Katie Wood • Janice Woodcock • John Woodlyn • Todd Woodward • Glenn Worgan • Jeffrey Wright • Chris Wurst • Jim Wyatt • Monica Wyatt • Adrienne Yancone • Amy Yaskowski • Neil Yersak • Carey Yonce • George Yu • Jing Yu • Oliver Yu • Zinat Yusufzai • John Zabilowicz • David Zaiser • Chuanming Zhang • Morris Zimmerman • Pamela Zimmerman

Partners

AIA Philadelphia • Alon Abramson • Delaware Valley Green Building Council (DVGBC) • Energy Coordinating Agency of Philadelphia, Inc. • The Food Trust • Local Initiatives Support Corporation, Philadelphia • NeighborhoodsNow • Pennsylvania Fresh Food Finance Initiative (FFFI) • Philadelphia Association of Community Development Corporations (PACDC) • Philadelphia Corporation for Aging • Philadelphia Department of Commerce • Philadelphia Industrial Development Corporation (PIDC) • Philadelphia Office of Housing and Community Development (OHCD) • Preservation Alliance of Greater Philadelphia • The Reinvestment Fund

Contributors

Maurice Cox
Associate Professor,
University of Virginia,
School of Architecture

Maurice is an urban designer, architectural educator at the University of Virginia's School of Architecture, and former mayor of Charlottesville, Virginia. He most recently served as Director of Design for the National Endowment for the Arts, where he presided over the largest expansion of direct grants to the design fields, oversaw the Governors' Institute on Community Design, Your Town: The Citizens' Institute on Rural Design, and the Mayors' Institute on City Design. Maurice served as a Charlottesville City Councilor for six years before becoming the mayor of that city, from 2002 to 2004. A recipient of the 2009 Edmund N. Bacon Prize, the Harvard University Graduate School of Design 2004–05 Loeb Fellowship, and the 2006 John Q. Hejduk Award for Architecture, he received his architectural education from the Cooper Union School of Architecture.

Alan Greenberger, FAIA
Deputy Mayor for Plan-
ning and Economic
Development and Direc-
tor of Commerce, City of
Philadelphia

Alan was appointed Philadelphia's Deputy Mayor for Planning and Economic Development and Director of Commerce by Mayor Michael Nutter in June 2010. Previously he served as Executive Director for the Philadelphia City Planning Commission, and was an architect and planner with MGA Partners and its predecessor, Mitchell Giurgola Architects.

During his thirty-four years in private practice, he was the principal designer on numerous architectural, urban design, and planning projects, including the Salvation Army Kroc Corps Community Center in Philadelphia, the West Chester University School of Music and Performing Arts Center, and the renovation of Lehigh University's historic Linderman Library.

Alan serves on the boards of several organizations, including the Fairmount Park Art Association, the Delaware River Waterfront Corporation, and the Philadelphia Industrial Development Corporation. He is also a cofounder of the Design Advocacy Group of Philadelphia, a fellow of the AIA, and a faculty member of the Department of City and Regional Planning at the University of Pennsylvania.

Sally Harrison, AIA
Associate Professor,
Temple University

Sally is a registered architect and Associate Professor of Architecture at the Tyler School of Art at Temple University. She is a former chair of the Department of Architecture and the director of the Urban Workshop, a university-based practice that seeks to address community design issues through a process of participatory site-specific research and design, collaborating with other place-making disciplines including landscape architecture, public art, planning, and geography. Sally has served on the board of the Philadelphia and Pennsylvania Chapters of the AIA, and was a founding member of the Community Design Collaborative.

Mark Alan Hughes
Distinguished Senior
Fellow, PennDesign and
TC Chan Center, University
of Pennsylvania
Associate Director, Policy,
Markets and Behavior,
Greater Philadelphia Innovation Cluster (GPIC)

Mark leads GPIC's research program aimed at understanding obstacles to adoption of energy-efficient building system technologies and the financial, policy, and regulatory instruments that speed technology adoption through increased ROI. Mark is also a Distinguished Senior Fellow of the University of Pennsylvania School of Design. As a cabinet member in the administration of Mayor Michael Nutter, he established the City's first Office of Sustainability, created a distinguished 20-member Sustainability Advisory Board, and designed and produced the City's 2015 policy framework—Greenworks Philadelphia, which presents fifteen ambitious targets for 2015. He also designed and led the City's strategy for maximizing the value and impact of federal resources under the American Recovery and Reinvestment Act. Mark graduated from Swarthmore College and received a PhD in Regional Science from Penn.

Don Matzkin, AIA
Founder, Community
Design Collaborative
Former Principal, Friday
Architects/Planners, Inc.

Don was born and raised in Philadelphia and attended Philadelphia public schools. After receiving his bachelor's degree from Cornell in 1963, he spent two years on active duty with the US Navy. Don left active duty status in 1965 and returned to Philadelphia, taking jobs with Murphy Levy Wurman; Montgomery, Bishop and Arnold; and finally Vincent G. Kling and Associates, before cofounding Friday Architects/Planners in 1970 with Peter Arfaa, David Slovic, and Arlene Matzkin. Don crafted a professional life around community service and design and helped found the Community Design Collaborative and the Charter High School for Architecture and Design. He retired from active practice in 2010.

Elizabeth K. Miller
Executive Director, Community Design Collaborative

Beth has served as Executive Director of the Community Design Collaborative since 2001, helping the organization evolve from a part-time, largely volunteer initiative of AIA Philadelphia into a full-service, independent nonprofit affecting design policy in the City of Philadelphia. With more than 20 years of experience in the fields of strategic planning, community development, and nonprofit management, she has held various positions with Fairmount Ventures, the National Trust for Historic Preservation, and Susan Maxman Architects. Beth was recently appointed by Mayor Michael Nutter as a member of the Philadelphia City Planning Commission. She has a master's degree in government administration from the Fels Institute of Government at the University of Pennsylvania and a bachelor's degree in the growth and structure of cities from Bryn Mawr College.

Brian Phillips, AIA, LEED AP
Principal, ISA (Interface Studio Architects, LLC)
Lecturer, PennDesign, Department of Architecture, University of Pennsylvania

Brian is founding principal of ISA, an award-winning architectural design and research office in Philadelphia. He has extensive design experience with a range of building scales, urban design, master planning, and speculative work. He has committed considerable energy to bringing innovative design projects to urban neighborhoods with strong environmental agendas. Brian holds a bachelor's degree from the University of Oklahoma and an MArch from the University of Pennsylvania. He has lectured widely on technology and urbanism, and his writing and design work have been featured in publications such as *306090*, *Dwell*, and *Metropolis*.

Brian received a 2011 Pew Fellowship in the Arts. He is a visiting professor at the Technological University of Monterrey in Querétaro, Mexico, as well as a lecturer at PennDesign at the University of Pennsylvania.

Todd Woodward, AIA, LEED AP
Principal, SMP Architects

Todd is a principal of Philadelphia-based SMP Architects, a nationally recognized leader in sustainable design, as well as an adjunct professor of architecture at Temple University. He served for several years on the Board of Directors of the Community Design Collaborative and currently serves on its Advisory Council. He also serves on the editorial board of *Context: The Journal of AIA Philadelphia,* and the board of the PennDesign

Alumni Association. Todd holds a BArch from Penn State and an MArch from the University of Pennsylvania. He is a lifelong Phillies fan.

Jess Zimbabwe, AIA, AICP, LEED AP
Executive Director, Daniel Rose Center for Public Leadership in Land Use, Urban Land Institute (ULI)

Jess is the founding Executive Director of the ULI Rose Center, an organization that offers leadership development, technical assistance, trainings, and research to support excellence in public sector land use decision making. Before joining ULI, she was the Director of the Mayors' Institute on City Design and an Enterprise Rose Architectural Fellow at Urban Ecology in San Francisco. She is past president of the Association for Community Design, and has served on several other nonprofit boards and committees.

Acknowledgments

For the Community Design Collaborative to influence Philadelphia's neighborhoods, we have needed leverage to gain advantage from numerous generous investments of time and resources. For more than 20 years the Collaborative has "leveraged" the pro bono services of **design** professionals, the commitment of **community** based-organizations, and the desire for **collaboration** among private, nonprofit, and public stakeholders. We have many to thank for helping us make this investment in the city's urban landscape.

We dedicate this book to the Collaborative's volunteers, whose combined efforts since 2001 have generated nearly $5 million dollars in pro bono preliminary design in service to the region's nonprofits; to the nonprofits that have the perseverance to work with the Collaborative to put their credible ideas to paper; to the public, private, and nonprofit developers who help projects take shape; and to the firms that continue this work into the built environment.

We are grateful to our partners at the Office of Housing and Community Development, in particular Belinda Mayo and Deborah McColloch, who saw the value of the Collaborative's technical assistance for neighborhood advisory councils, community development corporations, and other nonprofits serving low- and moderate-income neighborhoods. We thank AIA Philadelphia and Chapter Presidents for the foresight to connect its members to community service through the Collaborative and other nonprofit entities such as the Charter High School for Architecture and Design (CHAD) and the Center for Architecture.

In an era of scarce resources, the Collaborative has been fortunate to harness the urban energy of dedicated design professionals and community leaders. Many thanks to our partners at the William Penn Foundation, especially Shawn McCaney and Gerry Wang, for pushing us to move beyond responsive site-specific service grants to proactive initiatives that attract attention, action, and resources. Support from numerous family and corporate foundations has helped us sustain service over the past ten years, including: PNC Foundation, Bank of America, Carpenter's Company, Citizens Charitable Foundation, Claniel Foundation, Connelly Foundation, Counselors of Real Estate Foundation, Dolfinger-McMahon Foundation, Drumcliff Foundation, Samuel S. Fels Fund, the Walter J. Miller Trust, National Endowment for the Arts, The Philadelphia Foundation, Urban Land Institute Foundation, Union Benevolent Association, Henrietta Tower Wurts Memorial, and the Wells Fargo Foundation.

We are indebted to our Infill Philadelphia partners—NeighborhoodsNow, LISC Philadelphia, The Reinvestment Fund, and PIDC—who embraced the design challenge as a proactive, problem-solving process. Special thanks also goes to the Collaborative's "godfather," Don Matzkin, and our founders—too numerous to mention—for taking action toward social justice through design. We are grateful to our board, advisory council members, and co-chairs past and present: Mami Hara, Paul Marcus, Cece Denegre, Michael Paul, Lisa Armstrong, Susan Smith, Dan Garofalo, Howard Lebold, Stephen Gibson, Patrice Carroll, and Alice Berman, who have challenged their peers to raise the bar for civic engagement and action.

Heartfelt thanks to our able and dedicated staff: Heidi Segall Levy, Linda Dottor, Carryn Golden, Robin Kohles Harrison Haas, and Camille Cazon, for their deft ability to mobilize volunteers and nonprofits, and to recent Collaborative fellows and staff: Emily Stromberg, Haley Loram, and Erik Kojola. We are indebted to Susan Frankel, our founding director, and early staff member Jan Strouse, who developed a project management system for the first decade that we still use today. We also thank our consultants Don Kligerman of Fairmount Ventures and Sharon Gallagher of Sage Communications for their counsel.

Acting as an advocate, connector, and provider requires passion but also flexibility, due deference, and humor, and we were fortunate to assemble an editorial team for this project with these same qualities. The intrepid project manager Alison Rooney and Advisory Council champion Todd Woodward kept us focused on the task with humor and grace. Our staff and board took on the feat of winnowing our archives of more than 600 service grants down to a final list of 20, as curated by Linda Dottor. Our graphic designer Anthony Smyrski of Smyrski Creative made us look good with his clarity and inventiveness. In addition, we showcase here the talents of many photographers, including Mark Garvin, Peter Kubilis, Sam Oberter, Don Pearse, Wynne Levy, Jacob Helman, Haley Loram, Matt Wargo, Barry Halkin, Carryn Golden, and Raymond W. Holman, Jr.

Our colleagues near and far contributed thoughtful, provocative essays. Jess Zimbabwe and Maurice Cox put the Philadelphia story into a national context, and Mark Alan Hughes and Alan Greenberger talk about design advocacy at a new level. Don Matzkin and Sally Harrison renew the unwavering belief of the Collaborative founders that architects and affiliated professionals have a moral obligation to deliver pathways for social justice through design of the environment. Todd Woodward and Brian Phillips pose provocative questions and challenge our notions of public interest architecture, pro bono service, and advocacy.

And finally, we extend a special thanks to the Co-Chairs of our Board of Directors, Paul Marcus and Mami Hara, to our 20th Anniversary Steering Committee, led by Michael Paul, and to our Urban Energy Honorary Committee, which includes Phil Eastman, Beverly Coleman, John Grady, Alan Greenberger, John Claypool, and Andy Frishkoff. Each of them provided invaluable guidance as we created a year-long celebration of the Collaborative's past, present, and prospective future.